Date Due

The Girder Bridge
AFTER BRUNEL AND OTHERS

Brunel's Chepstow Bridge modernized. An express, diesel-hauled, crosses the first welded steel truss girder bridge on a British Railways' main line.

The Girder Bridge

AFTER BRUNEL AND OTHERS

by

P. S. A. BERRIDGE, M.B.E., F.I.C.E.

formerly Assistant Engineer (Bridges)
Western Region of British Railways

ROBERT MAXWELL · PUBLISHER

First published by Robert Maxwell : Publisher
4, Fitzroy Square, London, W.1
A division of Pergamon Press Ltd.

Printed in Great Britain by A. Wheaton & Co., Exeter

08   007095 7

To

OLGA

my wife and fellow-traveller across life's bridges

Contents

List of Plates

ix

Foreword

by H. SHIRLEY-SMITH, C.B.E., F.C.G.I., F.I.C., B.SC., F.I.C.E

THE first link that Stuart Berridge and I had in common was service in India, he was on the North-West Frontier as Deputy Chief Engineer, Bridges, for the North Western Railway—and I as Senior Engineer on the building of the Howrah Bridge in Calcutta. Since then we have frequently met as friends and colleagues. During his $17\frac{1}{2}$ years' work in this country, as Bridge Assistant to the Great Western, and latterly the Western Region of British Railways, he has carried out much important and original work.

Bridges are one of the engineers' most vital services to mankind. It is always a challenge—whether working in a highly developed country such as Great Britain, or in some remote river valley overseas—to sink the piers of a bridge to cross the river, to see the spans steadily stretching across from shore to shore, and, finally, to view the completed bridge and watch the traffic flowing over to promote and nourish industries on either side.

In this book, Stuart Berridge traces, in fascinating detail, the development of railway girder bridges in Great Britain for 140 years, from the start of the railway age in 1825—giving revealing glimpses of the working methods of Brunel, Robert Stephenson, Benjamin Baker and other giants of the past.

The story ends with an account, easily intelligible to the layman but also full of interest to the engineer, of the latest techniques used in the welded trusses and mighty spans of today.

Author's Preface

THIS book contains the story, hitherto untold, of the development of the girder bridge, product of the Industrial Revolution in Britain.

My interest in bridges was aroused at Whitgift Grammar School where a friendship with a descendant of the engineer who built the Forth Bridge, led, in 1918, to an apprenticeship with Sir William Arrol & Co., at Dalmarnock Iron Works, followed by a brief period with consulting engineers in Westminster. Subsequently, after spending twenty years in India, reconstructing and strengthening girder bridges on the North Western Railway, I came to the Great Western Railway where the post of Bridge Assistant gave me the chance to study, at first hand, some of the historic works of famous bridge engineers of the past.

Isambard Kingdom Brunel had been the first Chief Engineer at Paddington. I was privileged to serve under Sir Allan Quartermaine, C.B.E., M.C., the last Chief Engineer of the railway company; and, it was my good fortune to be entrusted with altering some of Brunel's great bridges.

It is not necessary to be an engineer to follow this story. There are no formulae, no sums. It is not a textbook, though the reasoning behind the choice of shape and form of the bridges, governed, as they were, by the materials and resources available at the time of construction, will not go unnoticed by the discerning student of structural engineering. It does not pretend to cover all aspects of bridge engineering; it is solely about the why and wherefore of trusses and plate girders, the men who made the bridges and put them up, the men who have been looking after them, and the improvements which have led to the enormous advances seen in bridge design at the present day.

A bridge is a monument to its creator. So, in this study of the behaviour of these monuments during a century and more of service, new light is thrown on the character and the craftsmanship of those pioneers who constructed the first long-span bridges for railways crossing wide estuaries on the coast of Britain. The masterpieces at Chepstow and Saltash reveal the genius of a railway engineer who was first and foremost a brilliant designer of bridges. Evidence, based on observations of the low cost and the high degree of reliability of the Royal Albert Bridge—the only surviving suspension bridge carrying railway trains—shows that, as an engineer, Brunel was far more enlightened than any of his contemporaries.

The reader seeking to find drama in these pages will be disappointed. The oft-repeated tale of the fall of the first Tay Bridge is not included. Nevertheless, the story is as fascinating as any other true record of human endeavour. With the reconstruction of Chepstow Bridge in 1962, this book includes a description of recent changes which have taken place in the conception of the girder bridge. There have been changes in almost every aspect; changes in design methods, in the steel itself, in the manufacture of girders, and in the ways of building them into the bridges; fundamental changes going deep down into the very heart of bridge engineering, yet going on almost unnoticed in this age of rapid scientific progress; changes which have culminated in the building of the Severn Road Bridge, the world's slimmest and most advanced steel structure.

Although many of the 62,640 bridges on British Rail (36,700 under the line, and 25,940 over it) have had their day, the lessons learned from the experiences of the builders of the great bridges of the past, and from those who have been engaged in looking after the girderwork, have been invaluable. Here, indeed, is a tale of which every British engineer has good reason to feel proud. It is a record of achievement that should not be forgotten.

Maidenhead, 1968

Acknowledgements

I AM grateful to Mr. H. Shirley-Smith for his kindness in writing the Foreword. He is one of the world's leading bridge engineers. In the past he has worked on the design or erection of every one of the longest spans in Great Britain, India, Africa and Australia. This year (1967) he is President of the Institution of Civil Engineers.

I thank all the consulting engineers and the contractors for their kind assistance on the sites of the great bridge constructions which it has been my good fortune to visit. At each, I have been made very welcome, and I have been allowed to use my camera freely.

I acknowledge the kind assistance of the members of my former office, the Steelwork Office of the Civil Engineering Department of the Western Region of British Rail at Paddington Station. To attempt to give names would be to run the risk of leaving someone out. I would not like to be guilty of doing that.

I am grateful to my former chief engineers, Sir Allan Quartermaine, a Past-President of the Institution of Civil Engineers, to Mr. M. G. R. Smith and Mr. F. R. L. Barnwell, for permission to include many interesting photographs taken from the railway records. And I include a word of praise to Mr. W. R. Macdonald, chief photographer on the Western Region, and his staff, for the high quality of the B.R. pictures.

I have made use of historic records preserved in the library at the Institution of Civil Engineers, and I do thank Mr. H. C. Richardson, head librarian, for his help in looking up references. To the President and Council of the Institution, I am grateful for the permission to publish extracts from the Minutes of the Proceedings.

I thank William Arrol Millar for kindly verifying facts about his great uncle, Sir William Arrol.

To Lieut. Colonel T. M. Simmons, the curator of the Science

Museum at South Kensington, I am grateful for permission to reproduce again the picture of the model of Gaunless Viaduct; it appeared previously, illustrating one of my writings for *Railway Steel Topics*, published by the United Steel Companies Ltd.

To *The Railway Gazette*, *The Engineer*, and *Engineering*, I make grateful acknowledgement for the reproduction in this book of several of my own photographs which have appeared in those periodicals.

CHAPTER 1

First Principles

THE world's first iron truss girder bridge carried the Stockton & Darlington Railway over the Gaunless stream at West Auckland in County
Durham. It had four spans, each 12 ft 6 in. long. The design has been attributed to George Stephenson, the engineer of the line. The fabricators
were John & Isaac Burrell of Orchard Street, Newcastle upon Tyne.

The Gaunless Viaduct was built before the S. & D.R. was opened
in 1825. It was taken down in 1901; and after being on show along with
the old engines "Locomotion No. 1" and the 0-6-0 "Derwent" at
Darlington station for a number of years, the ironwork of this historic
bridge has found a permanent home in the Railway Museum at York.

The girders of the Gaunless Viaduct are worthy of close study because of the ingenious way wrought iron bars used for the chords or
flanges were combined with cast iron pillars or verticals which served
to transmit the reactions from the track above, and to keep the curved
wrought iron bars in shape. Quite evidently, George Stephenson
appreciated the difference between the properties of cast iron and
wrought iron.

The two great "truss" spans of I. K. Brunel's masterpiece, the Royal
Albert Bridge across the Tamar at Saltash, bear a marked resemblance
in shape to the girders of the Gaunless Viaduct. This is because both
incorporate the common principles of the arch and the suspension
bridge. The upward curvature of the top chord (the rib of the arch)
matches the downward hang of the bottom chord (the suspension
chains), and, at the ends, the outward thrust of the former is balanced
by the inward pull of the latter. Every beam or girder which rests freely

1

on supports at each end of a single opening or span behaves in the same way. The top chord is under compression like the rib of an arch, and the bottom chord is in tension like the chains or cables of a suspension bridge; but the upward curvature of the former is not always so exactly mirrored in the downward curvature of the latter.

At Gaunless, the track was carried above the trusses. The distances between the cast iron pillars was just over 2 ft or about the same as the span of the rails between sleepers in the track. Stephenson used round wrought iron bars, 2½ in. in diameter and curved to the radius of a 24-ft diameter circle, for the chords of his trusses. These bars he threaded through holes in the bosses cast in the pillars; at the ends he united top and bottom chords in holes in common bosses in the vertical posts which formed the top of the round cast iron columns of the piers.

At Saltash, the track is carried on a plate girder bridge slung below the "trusses", each of which spans 455 ft. Brunel used a single oval wrought iron tube, 12¼ ft high and 16¾ ft wide, for the top chord which is common to two pairs of suspensions chains, forming the bottom chords. His pillars or verticals are of wrought iron and they extend below the trusses and carry the plate girder bridge. The Royal Albert Bridge was opened in 1859. It is significant that Brunel shunned the use of cast iron altogether in the trusses. Later on we shall see why.

Here, a short digression in the way of a simple explanation of how a bridge "works" will ensure a proper understanding of the engineering terms used in this book, and at the same time enable the non-technical reader to follow this fascinating subject. The theory of the way in which a simply-supported beam resists the tendency to collapse is the same no matter whether the beam is a plain baulk of timber, an I-shaped metal girder or a truss. The forces or stresses due to bending cause the top fibres to shorten and the bottom ones to lengthen; in other words, the top fibres are compressed and the bottom ones are stretched. It is easy to visualize this happening in the trusses of the Royal Albert Bridge where the tubes are compressed as they resist the inward pull of the chains.

In an arch with the ribs in compression, the end thrust is generally resisted by substantial foundations designed to transmit the vertical and horizontal reactions into the ground. So, in a way, an arch is like the compression half of a giant beam dependent upon the ground to resist the horizontal component of the reactions trying to push the skewbacks further apart. If the ground is too soft to stop the skewbacks sliding away from one another, a horizontal tie may be used to join the two foundations together. So the horizontal tie acts like the string of a bow.

The six 125-ft spans of the High Level Bridge at Newcastle upon Tyne demonstrate this principle of the bow-and-string. There are four cast iron arch ribs to each span and the whole of the end-thrusts from them are taken by wrought iron ties. On pillars above the ribs, there is a deck carrying three railway tracks; below, on a deck supported on hangers and the horizontal ties, there is a roadway flanked on either side by footpaths located between the arch ribs. The arrangement combines the cast iron in compression in the ribs with the wrought iron in tension in the ties so that, in effect, each span is a self-contained beam or girder-mechanism which does not transmit any horizontal thrust to the high piers supporting it. Described as Robert Stephenson's most famous work, the Newcastle High Level Bridge first carried trains on 15 August 1849; it was formally opened by Queen Victoria returning south from Scotland on 28 September. The piers are founded on timber piles and it is said to have been the first occasion when Nasmyth's steam-piling machine was used in a big way.

The bow-and-string principle is to be found in every beam or girder. In the parallel-flange beam, the curve of the "arch rib" and the curve of the "tie", the top and bottom flanges respectively, are of infinite radius; they are straight. The edges furthest from the middle are the most heavily stressed parts under the bending forces. If a flanged beam were to break through being overloaded by the bending forces, either the top flange would buckle because it could no longer stand the squeeze, or the bottom flange would tear apart because the metal could no longer sustain the tension imposed on it. A trussed beam would fail in just the same way; either the top chord would crumple or the bottom one fracture.

Bending stresses are greatest at the centre of a span when it is uniformly loaded throughout its length, and they dwindle to nothing over the bearings or supports at each end. That is why girders with curved chords or flanges are deepest at the middle. Girders with straight parallel chords or flanges are made so only in deference to the cost of manufacture; it is cheaper to have surplus metal in a flange than to fashion a rolled I-section beam with curved flanges.

The other principal forces acting on a beam or truss are caused by

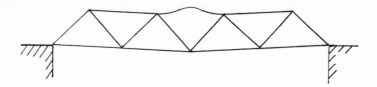

Compression (top) chord buckled by excessive bending

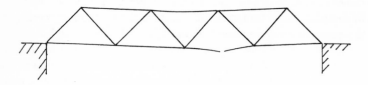

Tension (bottom) chord severed by excessive bending

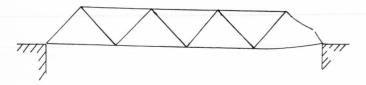

End diagonal web member failing through excessive shear

FIG. 1.

shear. Shear tends either to cleave a girder right through from top to bottom, or to split it into separate horizontal layers. Vertical shear is greatest at the end of a load. For instance, the shear caused by a load covering the whole span, will be a maximum at a point immediately on

FIG. 2. "Shear tends . . . to split a girder into separate horizontal layers"

the spanside of a bearing; and, on a railway bridge, the shear caused by the moving load will be greatest just in front of a uniformly-loaded train or immediately behind it.

Apart from the effects of wind, centrifugal forces, the weight of snow, etc., a bridge is expected to carry three principal forms of loading: the weight of itself, called the dead load; the weight of the train, called the live load; and impact which is the extra loading effect resulting from the way the live load is applied. A bridge must be strong enough to return to its original shape *exactly*, after the live load leaves it. A bridge will bend under the weight of a train. But, within limits, the amount a girder bends or deflects is of little consequence. The main point is that it must return to its original shape, no matter how many times the loading is applied. The only exception is in the case of the brand new riveted girder where some settling down of the parts may be expected under the first application.

If the superstructure of a bridge ceases to return to the shape it had before the passage of a train, some part of the girderwork will, in all probability, have been overstrained. In other words, some part of the iron or steel will have been over-loaded; and, after being relieved of the load, the metal has not enough strength to return to its former length. When a straight bar is stretched by an *overload*, applied so that all parts of the bar carry exactly the same amount of load, the bar will, after the load is removed, remain a tiny fraction longer than it was before the load was put on.

A beam behaves in the same way, except that the stresses to which its parts are subjected vary from the greatest stretch or tension on its bottom surface, to the greatest squeeze or compression on the top. So, if the bottom layer or fibre, as engineers like to call it, is overstrained, the effect, after the load goes away, will be for the remainder of the metal to try to restore the beam to its original shape. At the same time, the overstrained fibre is being made to follow suit. It is as though that fibre has been injured. Weakened, it no longer has sufficient strength to make the return. When the beam is loaded the next time, the overstrained fibre will not play its part in resisting the tendency of the beam to bend, and another fibre will be overstrained. Eventually, as more and more loads cross the beam, and more and more fibres are overstrained, the beam or girder will lose its camber and develop a droop or permanent sag, which will not disappear when the load goes away.

If, however, the load does not cause any overstraining at all, our straight bar will always return to its original length, after the load has been removed. And, similarly, the girder superstructure of a bridge, with no fibres overstrained, will return to its original shape after a train has passed.

Overstraining a piece of wrought iron or mild steel does not necessarily mean breaking it under a single application of loading. Mild steel, the kind of steel of which most girder bridges are made, will break when it is stressed to between 28 and 32 tons/in². But it can be loaded any number of times if the tensile stress is not allowed to exceed a figure of about $15\frac{1}{2}$ tons/in², and its strength will not be impaired. If, on the other hand, the loading causes higher stresses, the steel will have been overstrained and it will have lost some of its elasticity (i.e. its strength to return to its original shape and size). Iron, wrought but not cast, behaves in the same way though it is not nearly so strong. At best, wrought iron should not be subjected to repetitions of loading exceeding a stress of about 10 tons/in².

This very brief digression into the strength of materials will, it is hoped, give the new-comer to the subject an understanding of the mechanical properties of iron and steel sufficient to enable him to appreciate why some girder bridges wear out while others, which have been properly looked after and not allowed to rust, seem to last for ever.

CHAPTER 2

The Cast Iron Girder Bridge

IN 1847, the cast iron beam girder bridge was common wherever railways crossed canals or turnpike roads. The railway usually ran on a low embankment only a few feet above the surrounding country; in order to avoid steep or lengthy and costly gradients up to the crossings, the bridge constructions had to be made as shallow as possible. In other words, the C.D., the construction depth or thickness of the bridge measured from rail-level to the underside or soffit of the superstructure, had to be kept to a minimum.

An arch would have been preferred. With the ribs made of cast iron, it would have given a satisfactory kind of bridge; but where C.D. was restricted there was seldom room enough for the ribs of an arch below the railway. Some shallow form of beam having a straight level soffit was wanted. Timber was all very well for the very short span, but the wooden beam was limited by the girth and length of a tree trunk.

Malleable wrought iron was in production by 1821. George Stephenson showed his dislike of cast iron beams and used his influence to get wrought iron rails for the Stockton & Darlington Railway. By 1824, 20 out of the 25 miles of permanent way of the S. & D.R. had been laid with 12-ft and 15-ft lengths of wrought iron rails, weighing 28 lb to the yard, made by the Bedlington Iron Co. Reluctantly Stephenson had to complete the line with cast iron rails. These came from far-off South Wales. They were made by the Neath Abbey Iron Works, were fish-bellied in shape, in 4-ft lengths, and weighed 57½ lb to the yard.

It was a matter of cost. Cast iron beams (and a rail is a beam spanning from sleeper to sleeper) weighing more than twice their counterpart in

7

wrought iron and fetched from places more than a hundred miles away, were cheaper. The earliest wrought iron girder appears to have been used in a 31½-ft span road bridge near Glasgow in 1841. By 1845, quite large wrought iron box-section plate girders were being made for railways; but they were the exception and were used only for spans too long to be crossed with cast iron beams. For the bridge of medium span-length and restricted C.D., the cast iron beam was to continue to be built into bridge constructions on most of the railway lines, the Great Western Railway excepted, until 1882. The majority of those cast iron beam bridges gave satisfactory service, some remaining in the line today.

It was a pity the riveted wrought iron plate girder made a late start on railways; but, it was a product of the industrial awakening and as such it had to follow the coming of the railways which themselves created the demand for something more dependable than the cast iron beam. A cast iron beam suffers from a serious drawback; it gives hardly any warning of impending failure. Nowadays, by means of radiography, an internal flaw can be detected easily; but, in the heyday of railway construction in Britain in the nineteenth century, there was no known way of proving a cast iron beam except by test-loading it to see if it would break.

There was therefore an element of uncertainty about a cast iron beam bridge. More than one was to fail under traffic, trains being precipitated on to the roads below in 1882 and 1891.

Between 1830 and 1847 it was usual to have the cast iron beams tested before they left the foundry. This was called proving the beam. Raised up on wooden blocks at each end, the beam would be loaded with weights applied near the middle of the span. The amount of the test loads varied enormously, some engineers calling for loads inducing stresses equivalent to the effects of a loading three times greater than might be expected from the heaviest locomotive. Others stipulated the test loads should be six times more; and the most fastidious declined to accept a beam unless it had borne a test load ten times greater than it would have to bear in the bridge.

The wide range of test loading called for to prove a beam indicates something of the uncertainty that existed about the quality of these cast iron beams. But there was another unknown; namely the loading effect from a train crossing a bridge at speed. Frequent references in early records show that engineers were suspicious of the "concussions and vibrations" set up in a bridge as a train rumbled across; but at that time they had no means of measuring what the effect really was. Scant attention was paid to the balancing of the revolving and reciprocating parts of locomotives, and the wheel-load on the rail was often very different from the load assumed when a beam was being designed. Speed, of course, was to magnify this discrepancy in loading on bridges; and, in a number of cases the factor of safety of a bridge was a good deal less than the calculations showed.

At first the length of the span which could be bridged with a cast iron beam was limited by the size of beam the foundrymen could cast. A beam 40 ft long seems to have been about the limit for what could be regarded as a *sound* casting, though some engineers were prepared to accept beams more than twice that length. To meet the needs of longer spans, a particularly unfortunate form of trussed beam construction was evolved. For spans of about 100 ft, two or three cast iron beams were joined end to end, and at the joints they were given added support from trussing bars of wrought iron. In one form, the bars, nearly straight from end to end of the girder, were tightened giving a primitive prestressing effect to the cast iron; in others, the truss bars were inclined quite steeply up towards the ends like the chains in a suspension bridge.

The bridge with the single cast iron beam spanning from support to support was bad enough; the compound cast iron beam, as the multi-casting trussed beam was called, was a good deal worse. When a bridge of compound cast iron beams over the Dee near Chester collapsed under a passenger train a number of people were killed; and at the subsequent inquest on the victims, it was touch and go whether a charge of man-slaughter would not be brought against Robert Stephenson.

This accident happened on the evening of 24 May 1847 as a train to Ruabon was crossing the bridge. There were three right-hand skew spans each 108 ft long carried on stone piers and abutments; each opening was spanned with compound cast iron girders consisting of three castings trussed with wrought iron bars. It was the end left-hand casting of the span farthest from Chester which broke. The bridge carried the double-line of railway with separate superstructures for each track.

The engine had got safely across though there seems no doubt the girder actually broke when the driving wheels were at a point just beyond the joint between the middle and end castings of the girder. The tender was derailed, but it, like the engine, reached the safety of the

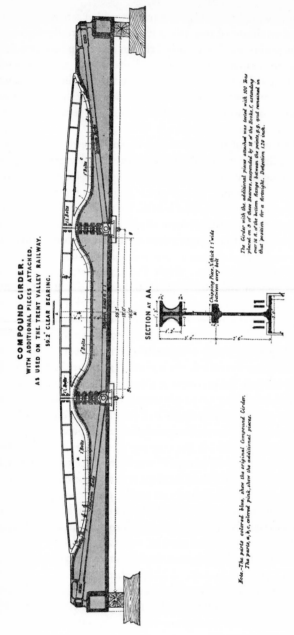

COMPOUND GIRDER,
WITH ADDITIONAL PIECES ATTACHED,
AS USED ON THE TRENT VALLEY RAILWAY.

59.2' CLEAR BEARING.

SECTION AT AA.

Chipping Piece, ⅝" thick 1 1" wide
between every bolt

*Note.—The parts colored blue, shew the original Compound Girder.
The parts, a, b, c, colored pink, shew the additional pieces.*

The Girder with the additional pieces attached was tested with 100 Tons placed on 8 of these Bearers, suspended by 18 of the bolts, f, extending over 16 ft. of the bottom flanges between the points, g, g, and remained in that position for a fortnight. Deflection 1.29 inch.

FIG. 3. Elevation and cross-section at the centre of a compound girder of a 60-ft span. The top castings were added after the Dee Bridge disaster of 1847.

far abutment. The coupling between the tender and the leading carriage snapped and the train was precipitated into the river. Of the thirty-five people in the train, five, including the fireman who was jerked off the tender when it was derailed, were killed; all the rest, except the driver who alone escaped scot free, were more or less seriously injured (MacDermot: *History of the Great Western Railway*, vol. 1, part 1).

The accident caused a tremendous furore in engineering circles; and Robert Stephenson, who was the engineer for the Chester & Holyhead Railway which included the Dee Bridge on the section between Saltney Junction and Chester then being used by the passenger trains of the recently completed Shrewsbury and Chester line, came in for some pretty harsh criticism.

To make matters worse, there had taken place at the Institution of Civil Engineers only a month before the Dee Bridge disaster, a discussion about the failure of a compound cast iron beam in a cotton-mill at Manchester. There, the beam had consisted of a single casting 31 ft 8 in. long (clear span) and 27 in. deep, and it had been trussed with wrought iron flats $2\frac{1}{2}$ in. $\times$ 1 in. which it was claimed increased the breaking load of the beam from 36 tons to 50 tons. Robert Stephenson had taken part in that discussion saying he had used cast iron trussed with wrought iron for railways of very considerable spans, in many instances exceeding 100 ft. "That over the Dee," he said, "was composed of girders of 108 feet span, each formed of 3 lengths of cast iron, trussed with wrought iron tension rods; all the girders were fully proved before they were erected; yet after the bridge had been open a few weeks, the cast iron of one of the girders broke through the bottom flanch [the old spelling of flange]. On examination, it was found that the truss rods had not been properly put on, and had afforded no assistance to the beam, until after the fracture took place, when the whole weight was brought upon them, which they bore perfectly, notwithstanding the vibration of passing trains, until the necessary repairs could be effected. Only one of the 12 girders, composing the bridge, exhibited any signs of weakness, and after the repair of that one, only very slight further alterations had been found necessary" (*Proc. Inst. C.E.*, vol. IV, 1847).

Small wonder the Government ordered a public enquiry into the use of iron in bridges. The findings of the committee who compiled the Report of 1847 shed some light on the art of bridge building for railways as it was practised 120 years ago. It makes fascinating reading.

CHAPTER 3

The 1847 Enquiry

THE Commission was appointed on 27 August 1847. The *Report of the Commissioners appointed to inquire into the Application of Iron to Railway Structures* was issued on 26 July 1849. In the preamble it had been thought expedient "for divers good causes and considerations, that a Commission should forthwith issue for the purpose of inquiring into the conditions to be observed by Engineers in the application of Iron in Structures exposed to violent concussions and vibration. . . . "

The members of the Commission were:

"Our Right Trusty and Well-beloved John Lord Wrottesley,
Our Trusty and Well-beloved Rev. Robert Willis, F.R.S., Clerk, Master of Arts, Jacksonian Professor in the University of Cambridge,
Henry James, Esquire, R.E., F.R.S., Captain in Our Corps of Engineers,
George Rennie, Esquire,
William Cubitt, Esquire, and
Eaton Hodgkinson, Esquire."

They were "to ascertain such principles and form such rules as may enable the Engineer and Mechanic, in their respective spheres, to apply the Metal with confidence, and shall illustrate by theory and experiment the action which takes place under varying circumstances in Iron Railway Bridges which have been constructed. . . . " The first of its kind in the world, the 1847 Report was to set the pattern for the future.

Up till then the proportions and forms employed for iron structures had been arrived at through experiment. Such tests as had been made were "by dead pressure", which was not the same thing at all. "From the nature of the railway system," ran the directive, "the structures are necessarily exposed to concussions, vibrations, torsions, and momentary pressures of enormous magnitude, produced by the rapid and repeated passage of heavy trains. . . . The disturbing causes, in a smaller degree, have always occurred in structures connected with mill-work or other mechanism."

It certainly looks as though the Commissioners had heard of the failure of the compound beam in the Lancashire cotton-mill.

Witnesses called to give evidence before the Commissioners included most of the leading civil engineers of the day. Brunel had at first objected to being called because he feared the ultimate recommendations of the committee would become binding. He rigorously opposed the laying down of rules or conditions to be observed in the construction of bridges lest "the progress of improvement tomorrow" might be embarrassed or shackled by recording and registering as law "the prejudices or errors of today". Others, including Robert Stephenson, agreed with Brunel. To their foresight and good judgement, the bridge-designer of modern times owes a debt for his freedom to use his ingenuity. Although specifications, bridge rules and so forth have become standard in many countries, they serve only to guide. The bridge engineer who departs from the rules is not necessarily guilty of breaking the law.

All lines except the Great Western Railway had adopted the cast iron beam bridge; Brunel alone had stood out against the practice of employing cast iron where it might be subjected to tension. He regarded it as an uncertain material of which castings of a very limited size only could be safely depended upon. But in spite of his strong views on the matter, Brunel, mindful of progress in the future, flatly refused to condemn the use of the cast iron beam outright. "Who will venture to say," he wrote in a letter to the Commissioners, "if the direction of improvement is left free, that means may not be found of ensuring sound castings of almost any form, and of twenty or thirty tons weight, and of a perfectly homogeneous mixture of the best metal? Who will say that beams of great size of such a material, either in single pieces or built, may not prove stronger, safer, less exposed to change of texture or to injury from vibration, than wrought iron, which in large masses cannot be so

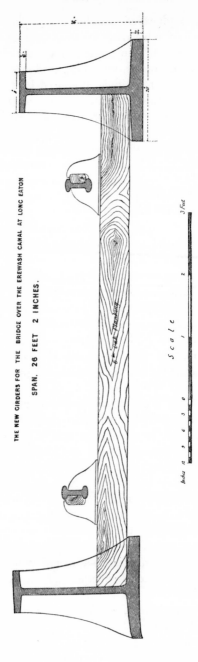

Fig. 4. Cross-section of a typical cast iron beam girder bridge used in the early days of railways in Britain. At the 1847 Enquiry, several eminent witnesses thought the torsional strain caused by resting the cross-bearers on the flanges of the cast iron beams could be ignored.

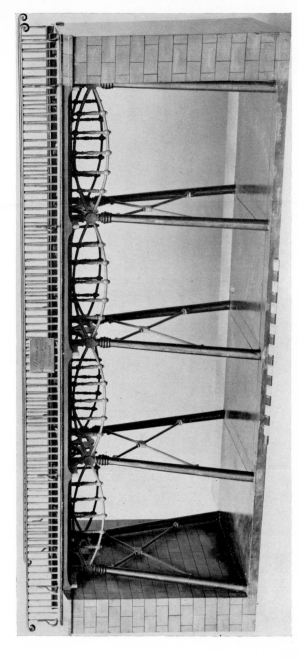

PLATE 1. Model of George Stephenson's Gaunless Viaduct on the Stockton & Darlington Railway (Crown Copyright, by kind permission of the Curator of the Science Museum at South Kensington).

PLATE 2. The twin 455-ft spans of the Royal Albert Bridge bear a marked resemblance in shape to the trusses of the Gaunless Viaduct. (Photo: B.R.)

PLATE 3. Stephenson used cast iron for the ribs of his 125-ft spans in the High Level Bridge at Newcastle upon Tyne.

PLATE 4. Brunel's 200-ft bow-and-string truss girders carrying the Windsor branch of the G.W.R. over the River Thames are of riveted wrought iron. Today, the single line of railway remaining across this old broad-gauge double-track bridge uses the half of the structure which has borne the kings and queens of England on their last journeys to St. George's Chapel. (Photo: B.R.)

homogeneous as a fused mass may be made and which when welded is liable to sudden fracture at the welds?" Brunel who tempered extreme caution with unmitigated audacity in the most original fashion, could afford such magnanimity.

Before 1847 it was customary for engineers ordering cast iron beams to specify a preference for a particular mixture of so much from Staffordshire, so much from Shropshire, South Wales, Newcastle or some other area. Although the ultimate breaking load of good sound cast iron in tension was known to lie between 7 and 10 tons/in², no minimum strength was mentioned in the order. The only concession to safety was the insistence that the beams should be proved under a test load before they left the foundry.

In the bridges, the cast iron beams of inverted T-shape in cross-section and having the top flange widened "to give extra lateral stability" would be loaded by timber cross-bearers (they hardly deserved the name of cross-girders) which rested on the *bottom* flanges. Efforts were made to seat the timbers well in against the webs of the beams; but as soon as the ends of the timbers became compressed, the reaction from these cross-bearers would be concentrated towards the very edge of the cast iron and the beams would be subjected to considerable torsion.

At the enquiry, several of the witnesses thought this torsional strain caused by loading the cast iron beams eccentrically could be ignored. Robert Stephenson declared, "The torsion is not enough to be noticed."

The Report issued after the close of the 1847 Enquiry gives a remarkably clear word-picture of the art of bridge engineering as it was being practised in those early days of railway construction in Great Britain and Ireland. The findings did put a stop to the use of the compound cast iron girder bridge in new lines, and most of the companies took early steps to either strengthen or reconstruct bridges incorporating trussed cast iron beams. But the girder made of a single casting was to live on, and bridges of this sort of construction were to go on being perpetuated right up to 1882. It was only after an express from Brighton to London Bridge had fallen through a cast iron girder bridge at Norwood Junction in 1891 that the Inspecting Officer of the Board of Trade recommended the reconstruction of all such underline bridges.

CHAPTER 4

The Witnesses

THE leading civil engineers called to the 1847 Enquiry included: Robert Stephenson, M.P., Joseph Locke, John Hawkshaw, John Urpeth Rastrick, Charles Fox, the Barlows, Peter William and William Henry, William Fairbairn, Joseph Glynn, Charles Heard Wild, Edwin Clark, the Cubitts, Joseph and Thomas, and Isambard Kingdom Brunel.

The scene was set in Gwydyr House in Whitehall. The time was November with the fog rolling in from the river close by; and the road muddy and paved only at street corners where crossing-sweepers expected a copper or two for sweeping the stones clean of horse-droppings.

Rastrick was the first witness called. It was Thursday 25 November 1847; Lord Wrottesley was in the Chair.

CHAIRMAN   You are a civil engineer?
RASTRICK   Yes.
CHAIRMAN   Have you acted very long in that capacity?
RASTRICK   Yes, almost all my lifetime.

Rastrick told how he had made cast iron beams 35 ft long for Buckingham Palace in 1821. On these he had carried out tests and the results had been published in a government "Blue Book". And some beams 41 ft long he had made and used to span the roof of the library in the British Museum, were described as the first large iron bearers that were ever made use of in London. One of his bridges was the road bridge over the Wye river at Chepstow which stills carries the A48 traffic today though the five arches have been strengthened with the addition

16

of steel joist ribs. In the course of his evidence, Rastrick gave some interesting facts about this historic bridge. He had been questioned about the possible effects of changes of temperature, and he was giving his opinion. "The roadway of the Chepstow Bridge stands about north and south; in the morning the sun came very full upon one side of the bridge, and those arches would get up; the bridge would have a small inclination across the roadway. As the sun went round, those came down, and when it got up on the other side, the other side got up. I tried experiments upon that bridge, and I found that the expansion and contraction were always the same at the same temperature; it always rose up and went down uniformly. . . . The difference between the effects of the hottest day in summer and the coldest day in winter was two inches rise in the centre of that arch." In fact, the arch has a rise of 12 ft at the centre and the span is 120 ft.

As a railway engineer, Rastrick is probably best remembered for his part in building the London Brighton & South Coast Railway, the line from London Bridge to Brighton having been opened on 21 September 1841; it included his monumental brick masonry viaduct which still carries trains high across the valley of the Sussex Ouse.

The next witness was John Hawkshaw, a civil engineer of twenty years' standing. He had been using Low Moor iron plates for riveted girders for 18 months; but apart from a dislike of building up compound girders out of little pieces of cast iron, he told the Commissioners he would be quite prepared to make simple cast iron girders for spans 100 ft. long. He evidently appreciated the uncertainty that surrounded the weights of trains crossing the bridges. Engineer of the Manchester & Leeds Railway, and later to become Sir John, he said: "Engineers can scarcely be certain of the load which may have to come upon their bridges. We all know that the weight of locomotive engines has been increased from 9 tons, which was the weight that I first began to use them at, up to 23 tons, and their speed also. Consequently, there is a very great degree of uncertainty in ascertaining the load to which bridges will be subjected. I should now make girders bear a larger proportion to the stress which may come upon them than I should have done formerly; and the rule which I propose to adopt in future with respect to girders is to make the strength about seven times the load; that degree of strength bears a very large proportion to the load; but I propose to do it, because the amount of money which is expended on girders on most railways is not a large sum. You do not adopt them at all where you can help it, and any saving which you effect by making the girders light, bears but an infinitesimal proportion to the whole cost of the works; therefore I think it is better to err on the safe side."

Hawkshaw was also engineer of the Wakefield, Pontefract and Goole Railway, and he gave a note about a compound trussed cast iron beam bridge "similar to the Dee Bridge but stronger" which carried the Goole line over the Knottingley ship canal. It was a bridge with a span of 89 ft. "The last time I was there," Hawkshaw told the Commissioners, "we ran a very heavy locomotive (about 22 tons) over it at 50 miles an hour, and I observed that the deflection was about half an inch. I propose to stiffen that bridge, because it is one of compound girders; and as it is of large span, and it is easy to double its strength, I propose to do so."

Quite obviously, the fall of the Dee Bridge had spread a feeling of uneasiness in the minds of engineers who had compound cast iron beam bridges on their lines. The more they learned about the behaviour of their bridges, the more uncertain they felt. The effect of speed exercised the Commissioners, and it seems that most of the witnesses expected deflections to increase as speeds rose, and the reason given was almost always laid on the bad effect of the rail joints. In one case an experiment had been tried with the head of the rails white-washed, and as a train was run across at speed it was noticed that lengths of the rails measuring no less than 5 in. had been left untouched on the trailing side of some of the joints.

Asked if he thought the weight could pass so quickly over a girder bridge as not to give sufficient time for deflection, Hawkshaw replied certainly not. Continuing he said: "If you could imagine the surface to be perfect, without any irregularity whatever, it is possible that if you were to run, say 1,000 miles an hour, you might get rid of a little deflection; but taking things practically, knowing that those surfaces are all very imperfect, you merely increase the force of impact by increasing the velocity." He was then asked: "In passing over thin ice with considerable velocity you are supported by it, which you could not be if you remained stationary?" Evidently ice-skating was indulged in out-of-doors in those days to a greater extent than it is today. Whether Hawkshaw was an expert skater we do not know, but his answer gives the impression that it was a sport with which he was on familiar terms.

He replied: "Yes, but you get a better surface upon thin ice than in the other case; and in the case of ice, time has to be afforded for the displacement of the water before the ice can break; the cases are not parallel."

Hawkshaw told the members of the enquiry he was introducing tubular girders of malleable iron in preference to cast iron beam bridges. "There is this advantage in wrought iron girders, that they would give you a little more warning than cast iron."

Charles Fox came next. He told the Chairman he had been a civil engineer for seventeen years, and during five years he had been an assistant under Robert Stephenson on the building of the London & Birmingham Railway. Subsequently as a contractor, he had designed and constructed many girders of large size and span for railways.

While content to begin to use compound trussed cast iron beam girders for spans exceeding 50 ft, he thought there were very few cast iron girders, ten years old, "which are not swagged". He believed the deflection due to the live load would gradually increase and never stop until the shape of the girder would resemble a festoon, and ultimately all girders would have to be exchanged. But at the same time he thought any loss of strength would be inappreciable and that the life of the bridge would depend on the mass of the material in the bridge compared with the weight of the train. In other words, where the ratio of the live load to the dead load borne by the structure was small, the bridge would have a longer life.

Speaking of his experience of riveted wrought iron girders, Fox mentioned a public road bridge over the River Lea near Hertford where, in spite of the passage of "constantly very heavy vibratory loads going over them, they were in perfect order".

Questioned about his opinion of the effects of speed, Fox said he would call 30 miles an hour pretty high. "I think," he said, "as you increase the speed you reduce to some extent the deflection; and I imagine it arises, in a great measure, from the short time there is to overcome the *vis inertiae* of the mass; of course the higher the velocity, the less time is expended in the train passing over the bridge."

Fox underlined the need for regularizing the "fixed principles in the structure of railway bridges". "One engineer," he said, "has thought the load should be so much; another has thought it ought to be two or

three times as great. I know that at the same moment I have had girders
under construction where the amount of proof per foot linear has varied
from six to one."

Peter William Barlow was the next civil engineer called. He had
been engaged on the South Eastern Railway. He seemed reluctant to
venture an opinion on the cast iron girder bridges on that line. Instead,
he confined his remarks to an invitation and offer to carry out experiments; and subsequently, a number of deflection readings were taken
on an eight-year-old bridge over the turnpike road south of Godstone.
Barlow confessed to a preference for girders wholly of wrought
iron, but found it too expensive. He thought the best idea would be
to make girders with a mixture, i.e. with wrought iron webs and
bottom flanges stiffened with cast iron in the top flanges.

William Fairbairn, questioned on 27 November 1847, made one of
the most enlightened contributions to the Enquiry. With upwards of
thirty years' experience and the successful building of the first of the
two great tubes for the Conway Bridge behind him, this was not sur-
prising.

Fairbairn showed an advanced understanding (for those days) of the
effects of loading a cast iron beam eccentrically. "Supporting the load
on one side of the flange is wrong in principle," he said, "and to a
certain extent, injurious in practice: but that method has many con-
veniences, and in practice we are frequently called upon to abandon
self-evident principles, in order to meet the requirements of different
structures. Under such circumstances, when the load is on one side of
the girder, the flange should be carefully constructed in order to bring
the bearing of the cross-beam as much as possible into the centre or
vertical plane of the girder." He showed sketches of cast iron cross-
beams resting on a ledge cast adjacent to the web on the main girder;
and in the case of timber cross-beams he suggested the flange of the
main girder next to the cross-bearers "to have small projections at
each cross-beam for the purpose of bolting them to the girder, and
thus unite the whole of the cross-beams and girders together". Here
was the first attempt, crude as it was, to unite the main girders and the
decking of a half-through type bridge in one homogenous U-frame.

Asked if he would advocate making cast iron girders with openings
in the webs, Fairbairn said: "I am of opinion that in cast-iron girders
such a process, if not fatal, would be, to say the least of it, exceedingly

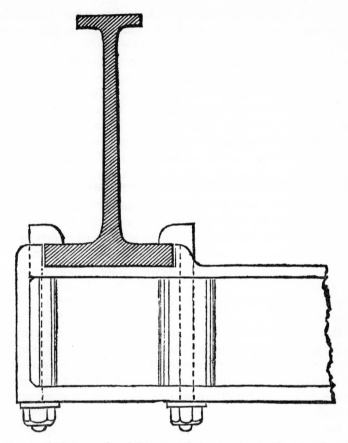

FIG. 5. Fairbairn preferred "to suspend the cross-beam, if made of cast iron, by hook bolts".

injurious. I have decided objections to anything like perforations in cast-iron girders, and it is even with some reluctance I would have a bolt-hole through the neutral axis unless thickened so as to compensate for the part taken out; besides, it is exceedingly objectionable to cut off the connection between the two resisting flanges of a girder, or to damage in any way a casting of this description. There is nothing I should be more tenacious about than the cutting or boring of any part of a well-proportioned girder, and I believe there is nothing so dangerous in the hands of persons unacquainted with the laws which govern the strengths of these important structures." One might be forgiven for suspecting Fairbairn had hit upon the need for avoiding stress-raisers— the cry of the twentieth-century designers of the all-welded plate girder! But actually, Fairbairn had in mind an even greater and more far-reaching axiom, namely the importance of simplicity in girder design. Asked if he objected to openings in the web on the lines of such a practice resulting in inferior castings, he said: "Certainly not, but from the considerations of more importance, namely the complexity of such a girder, and the additional material which you would require to give it the same security as regards strength. Again, I am a strong advocate for *simplicity of construction in everything*, and would on no account allow a distortion of form unless under circumstances which were inevitable." No doubt with this call for simplicity in mind, Fairbairn got over the need for drilling holes in the main girders by suspending the cross-beams from the bottom flanges. "The greatest care must be observed," he said, "not to perforate the bottom flange, but to suspend the cross-beam, if made of cast iron, by hook bolts. I have adopted this plan for many years with great success, and have never found it fail."

Later Fairbairn submitted a written report describing the strength, elasticity, and other properties of wrought iron girder bridges, as applicable to railways and other structures. Representing as it did the first major break-through in the establishment of the riveted plate girder, extracts from this report are so important that they are quoted herewith:

"The idea of crossing the river Conway and the Menai Straits on the line of the Chester and Holyhead Railway (two of the most formidable barriers ever presented to the engineer) properly belongs to Mr R. Stephenson.

"To carry this into practice required the united skill of the mechanical as well as the civil engineer; and it is highly gratifying to find that the successful completion of the first of the Conway tubes has not only attained that object, but it has established a new era in the history of bridges by the development of the properties of a hitherto untried material, and enables the engineer of the present day to conquer obstacles which, at no very distant date, were considered insurmountable.

"An undertaking of such importance to the scientific world, to the public, and to those more immediately interested, involves heavy responsibilities on the engineer, and before anything definite could be accomplished, it became absolutely necessary to institute a series of experiments to determine the practicability of such a structure, including other inquiries into the proportions and other properties of the tube. At the request of Mr Stephenson I had the honour of being selected to conduct this inquiry.

"Experiments on circular, elliptical, and rectangular tubes were accordingly undertaken; but it soon became evident from the results obtained that those of a rectangular form were best calculated for the purpose. It was not, however, until I had adopted the tube with the corrugated top that the real value of the tubular form became apparent, and, in fact, absolutely requisite in that part to offer sufficient resistance to the crushing force.

"I will not trouble the Commissioners with the details of the experiments, but simply state that it evidently became necessary to adopt some other shape than those of the circular and elliptical kind, and so to proportion the top and bottom sides of the tube as to effect a balance of the resisting forces of extension and compression, and thus to ensure the maximum force of resistance in every part. These proportions were clearly indicated by the rectangular form; and the formation of cells on the top side gave more effective powers of resistance to the crushing force than had been heretofore accomplished by the single plate.

"The discovery of the cellular top, and the greatly increased value which a tube thus constructed gave to the experiments, at once suggested a modified form of tubular girder adapted to shorter spans. This description of the bridge is now becoming general; and from its superior powers of resistance, greater security, and its adaptation to almost every description of span, we may reasonably infer that wrought iron is cheaper and safer, if not equally durable with any other description of material. It may, and I have no doubt it will, be urged, that wrought iron is more subject to oxidation and decay than cast iron or stone, a circumstance which cannot be disputed; but that can only arise from gross negligence on the part of those having charge of the structure, as two coats of good paint, every three years, will effectually protect it, and render it durable for almost any length of time.

"Besides, the girders as now constructed are accessible in every part, and, by careful attention, I can see no resaon why they should not last 500 instead of 50 or 100 years. Another objection brought against this description of bridge is, the risk of the rivets becoming loose; and from the number of joints, the whole is considered, by some as dangerous and insecure. Now, as regards this objection, no real weight can be attached to it, as the parties raising it cannot be acquainted with the nature and solidity of the work. It is next to impossible for a single rivet to get loose (unless the work is improperly executed); and, in the whole of my experience, I am not acquainted with any description of jointing so certainly secure and so well adapted to resist any description of strain as that of riveted plates. I speak practically and unhesitatingly on this subject: and I have only to instance steam-boilers, iron ships, and other vessels subjected to severe strains, as examples of the strength and tenacity of riveted plates; in fact, rivets seldom or ever get loose, but retain their position under every species of strain, and become as it were integral parts of the structure in common with the plates themselves."

The perseverance with experiment after experiment to determine the best proportioning of the various parts of the wrought iron girders so that the factor of safety against failure would, under the particular design load, be the same in the flanges and the web, showed an insistence that the ultimate form of the construction should make the most economical bridge possible. This is, of course, the endeavour of every engineer worthy of his profession.

The contributions made by Fairbairn and Stephenson with the bridge at Conway, and by Brunel with his at Chepstow were outstanding in the development of riveted wrought iron girder bridges. Later, we shall see why; but, the story is a fascinating one which would be spoiled if we were to omit to tell of the troubles with girders made of cast iron which were to daunt the railways almost up to the dawn of the twentieth century.

CHAPTER 5

"A Certain Degree of Oversight"

Joseph Locke, most celebrated of George Stephenson's pupils and incidentally driver on the footplate of the "Rocket" when the unfortunate Huskisson was run down on the day of the opening of the Liverpool & Manchester Railway, was 43 when he was called to give evidence.

Asked by the Chairman to give an account of his previous experience, Joseph Locke said he had been a civil engineer all his life. "I was educated in it," he said, "I was the resident engineer on the Liverpool & Manchester Railway during its construction from 1826 to 1830. I afterwards constructed the Grand Junction or Liverpool and Birmingham line, the South-Western line, the Sheffield and Manchester line, the Lancaster and Preston line, the Lancaster and Carlisle, the Caledonian and Scottish Central, the Scottish Midland, the Glasgow Paisley and Greenock, and various others."

Locke was regarded as a leading man in his profession. He certainly had not let the grass grow under his feet. Ten years after the 1847 Enquiry, Joseph Locke, F.R.S., M.P., was to succeed his friend Robert Stephenson as President of the Institution of Civil Engineers. It seems reasonable therefore to regard the evidence he gave at the 1847 Enquiry as being typical of a railway civil engineer of the day.

Asked if he thought the amount of deflection caused by a passing train might be injurious to a bridge, Locke was gloriously non-committal. "My notion is with reference to the testing of a beam," he said, "that if it had more deflection than you liked for a certain weight (although perhaps by going on with that weight you might break the beam) you would not like to use that beam though it might be unquestionably strong enough."

When it came to a question of the weights of locomotives running
on his lines, Locke seems to have been even less in touch with reality.
Asked what he considered to be the greatest weights which were then
passing over railways, Locke said: "We generally calculate the engine
at 30 tons; they are about 30 feet in length, and the heaviest now made
is 24 or 26 tons, we always say 30 tons; that is the greatest weight that
can come upon a railway, one ton for every foot in length; in ordinary
computations we take a sufficient margin. I am objecting now to engines 22 tons, and trying to keep them down to 18 or 20."

Told the Midland Railway was ordering engines of 32 tons weight
on four wheels with the axles 16 ft apart, Locke expressed great
astonishment, "I think it cannot be," he said, "I would not consent to
its running on any railway of mine."

If the Commissioners had any doubts about the "security" of bridges
carrying passenger trains, Locke can have done little to dispel such fears.
"If you would allow me to offer you one suggestion," he said, "it
would be this; that in all cases where cast iron is to be used, allow an
arch instead of a flat girder. I never would employ a flat girder of any
kind unless I was obliged to do so, because do what you will, the effect,
however slight it may be, of vibration of trains passing over flat girders,
let them be composed of what they may, is to separate the parts, and
ultimately to destroy them. I do not wish to excite alarm by this
opinion; for the time may be very remote indeed when that destruction
may take place. In the shape of an arch the parts are always clinging
the faster together. It is nothing but the requirements sometimes forced
upon me that induce me to construct a flat bridge; therefore I suggest
that if a general rule is to be adopted, let it be in favour of the arched
form of bridge."

When the Chairman asked Robert Stephenson if he was a civil
engineer, the answer was "Yes". He had been one for 23 years. Asked
to list some of the more important railway works he had been engaged
upon, Robert said: "The London and Birmingham was the first great
work which I had to execute; afterwards the continuous lines of railway
up to Berwick, including the North Midland, Birmingham to Derby,
the York and North Midland, the Newcastle and Darlington, and
the Berwick and Newcastle. . . . Always as engineer-in-chief."

Questioned about the truss-girder of the form used in the ill-fated
Dee bridge, Robert quoted the case of a number of "bridges I have

built upon the plan of the Dee girder-bridge". He showed a drawing and said he had added the three corresponding castings on the top of the original ones "so as to correct that which I admit to have been a certain degree of oversight". Continuing, he explained that in the previous arrangement, the reaction from the wrought iron truss-bars had actually increased the tension in the lower part of the cast iron in the two end castings. The report is not very clear; but evidently, by adding the upper layer of castings, Robert was endeavouring to make sure the pull from the wrought iron truss-bars would have the effect of hogging the end castings. To add to the confusion in the report, the drawing which Robert exhibited before the Commissioners and which belonged to some bridge he was designing for the Leopold Railway, showed the bottom castings shaped, and presumably machined for fitting with the upper castings; yet, Robert specifically described the addition of the upper row of castings as being additional pieces attached to an old bridge.

There is no doubt that a number of these compound trussed cast iron beam girder bridges were strengthened after the Dee bridge scare. Though only a span of 60 ft, the arrangement used on the Trent Valley Railway appears to have been typical. To have obtained an accurate fit between the upper and lower castings must have been one of the miracles of the age, and we are left in no doubt about the sigh of relief which the country must have experienced when the last of these monstrosities went to the scrap heap.

One other piece of evidence given by Robert Stephenson which is relevant to our story concerns the use of suspension bridges for railways. Although railway bridges were to continue to be built on the suspension principle for a number of years (and indeed the Royal Albert Bridge over the Tamar is a form of suspension bridge which still carries railway trains today, and we are told the mighty Tagus Bridge is to carry electric suburban trains one day in the future) few engineers of the twentieth century will disagree with Robert Stephenson's views. He said: "I do not think that a railway bridge could be made on the suspension principles; we have one at Stockton, which I replaced . . . and it was fearful when the engine went on to it. I have been informed that the wave on the bridge was 2 feet high. I do not say that from having seen it myself, but I have heard it stated, that when the engine and train went over the first time, that there was a wave before the

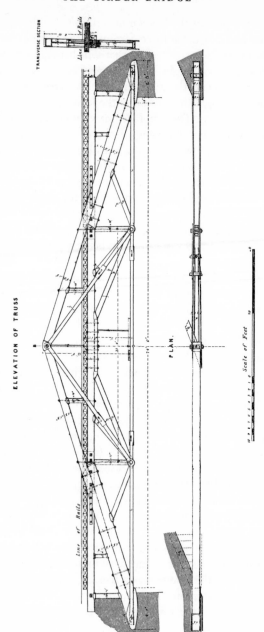

FIG. 6. One of Brunel's timber trusses with a span of 75 ft at St. Mary's Viaduct on the Cheltenham & G.W. Union Railway. A combination of Oregon pine and wrought iron, it was typical of his medium length bridges built before 1847.

engine of something like 2 ft, just like a carpet." The bridge over the River Tees at Stockton had been built by a Captain Brown, an early pioneer in suspension bridges, for the Stockton & Darlington Railway extension to Middlesbrough. It had a span of 300 ft, and describing the opening, Robert Stephenson had written: "Immediately on opening the suspension bridge for railway traffic, the undulations into which the roadway was thrown, by the inevitable unequal distribution of the weight of the train upon it, were such as to threaten the instant down-fall of the whole structure." History relates that the Stockton suspension bridge continued to carry trains of trucks of coal until it was replaced by Robert in 1842, but no locomotive ever again ventured on to it, the trucks being either pushed on from one end and pulled off at the other, or as seems more likely, they were hauled across by horses.

I. K. Brunel was shrewd in his replies to the Commissioners. When asked if he would condemn "the whole race of compound (trussed cast iron beam) girders", he remarked: "By no means. But I should observe generally in answer to this question, that I avoid the use of cast iron whenever I can, and that my experience, therefore is more limited than that of any other engineer probably. In all cases, where it is beyond a certain span of about 35 to 40 feet, I should prefer using timber or wrought iron, or the two combined." And at this stage he showed the Commissioners a drawing of one of his masterpieces in trussed timber, a 74-ft span of the St. Mary's Viaduct on the Cheltenham & G.W. Union Railway.

Brunel, championing the broad gauge and always jealous of his freedom of ideas, was in many ways diametrically opposed to the Stephensons. Ranking with the greatest of the engineers who have made civilization what it is today, Brunel was the genius developing ideas in a way all his own. But, talented as he was, Brunel was generous and liberal-minded, ever anxious to help a rival. Robert Stephenson was his rival and also his friend. Throughout his evidence, Brunel exercised discretion. He was careful not to say a word against the practices of his professional colleagues although it was patently obvious he must have been well aware of the folly of their ways.

Turning to the use of hot-driven rivets used in joining wrought iron plates together, Brunel voiced an opinion which, differing from the assumed principles used in design during the next hundred years, was in fact the *modus operandi* of the high-strength friction-grip bolted joint, the modern fastening pioneered on the Western Region of British Railways as recently as 1948. So important was Brunel's deliberation that it should be recorded in full. Here it is.

"I believe that in riveting plates together where they (the plates) will be exposed to tension, the rivets should not be considered as pins or bolts to be exposed to a cross strain, and holding the plate through which they pass merely as a bolt through the eye of a link, but they should be treated, and disposed accordingly, as clamps which compress the plates powerfully together, and produce an adhesion laying hold of the surface of the enclosed plate as if in a vice; to produce this effect the rivets must be of large diameter, which is well known to make the strongest work, and the workmanship generally must be good; but with proper precautions and the rivets judiciously disposed, and by crossing the joints of the different plates I believe there is hardly any limit to the approach which may be made to obtaining the entire strength of the plates, and such riveting, I believe, will be entirely unaffected by ordinary vibration or by oxidation."

Questioned about his experience with suspension bridges, Brunel said that up to that time he had not erected any for carrying railways, but he did think the suspension principles were applicable for railway purposes "under very peculiar circumstances".

Later, as though to prove his point, Brunel was to span the Wye at Chepstow and the Tamar at Saltash with his suspension bridges. The latter, the Royal Albert Bridge now well past its centenary and the sole surviving suspension bridge on a main-line railway, was exceptional. Today, it is unique.

CHAPTER 6

Inverythan

"THE grave calamity which befell the structure, now known as the 'Old Tay Bridge', occurred on the night of December 28th, 1879." So runs the second paragraph of the paper entitled "The Tay Viaduct, Dundee", read before the Institution of Civil Engineers on 8 May 1888. The members had met to hear a description of the new Tay Bridge. It was the first of the great riveted girder bridges which were to vindicate the sorely damaged reputation of the bridge engineers in this country.

Nevertheless, whenever the words "Tay Bridge" are mentioned today, it is not the present railway bridge which comes first to mind. To most people the words recall that frightful catastrophe when a whole train with 74 souls was swept into the storm-swept waters of the Firth as about 3000 ft of the first bridge fell over in the wind. The episode has been dramatized in books galore, and it is not the object of this writer to repeat the account of a fearful happening of which no one can possibly feel proud. The Tay Bridge disaster outshines in horror almost every other accident there has ever been which has been caused by bad bridge design and bad bridge construction. It was the longest railway bridge in the world and the accident resulted in one of the heaviest death rolls up to that time. It shook the engineering profession to its very foundations.

Chronologically, the Tay Bridge disaster of 1879 comes next to the wretched Dee Bridge failure which caused such a rumpus in 1847. Yet neither the findings of the 1847 Report nor the frightening news of the fall of the Tay Bridge appear to have had any effect on the continued use of the cast iron beam railway bridge. Hundreds more were to be

built before two more serious accidents finally put a stop to the dangerous practice. After the first which happened at Inverythan in 1882 the
use of cast iron beams in bridges on new constructions was prohibited.
After the second, at Norwood Junction in 1891, serious consideration
was to be given to the removal of all the cast iron girders from existing
lines.

Thirty-five years after the Chester to Ruabon evening train had
fallen into the Dee, the afternoon up mixed train from Macduff to
Inveramsay fell down on to the turnpike road at Inverythan. This
accident on the Great North of Scotland Railway happened at 4.57
p.m. on 27 November 1882. Just as at the Dee Bridge in 1847, the
engine got safely across the falling superstructure at Inverythan and the
tender remained attached to the engine though all the wheels were off
the rails. The train from Macduff consisted of five loaded waggons,
a brake van, two third-class carriages, one first-class, and one third-class
brake. According to a report in *The Railway Engineer* of the day, four
passengers were killed on the spot, while fourteen other passengers and
the assistant guard were injured, four of them seriously.

The railway at Inverythan was a single line and it had been opened in
1857. The bridge which had been in place since the line was opened,
consisted of two longitudinal cast iron girders, 38·9 ft in length and 3 ft
deep at the centre, each cast in two halves. Cross-bearers of creosoted
timber, new in 1871, were 10 ft long and rested upon the bottom
flanges of the main girders. These cross-girders were spaced 3 ft apart,
and above them were laid the longitudinal timbers to which the rails
were secured.

According to the report made by Major Marindin, the Board of
Trade Inspecting Officer of Railways, "the immediate cause of this
terrible accident was at once apparent upon the examination of the
fallen superstructure of the bridge". The cast iron girder carrying the
east side of the bridge was found to be broken into two nearly equal
portions, the fracture being in the southern half of the girder. Like at
the Dee, it was the trailing piece of beam which broke; but, instead of
the beam being in three pieces "trussed" with wrought iron bars, at
Inverythan the beam had been made in two pieces and merely joined
at the middle of the span by some arrangement of wrought iron bolting.
Whether these bolts were in tension or shear, is not clear.

The beam which broke had a vertical fracture close to the back of the filleting on the vertical joint flange, extending through the web from the bottom to the underside of the top flange, and there breaking out horizontally through the vertical flange. In the bottom flange the fracture had passed round the outer rim of the boss, and then across the flange, being 9 in. from the face of the joint at the inside and 6½ in. at the outside, and having the edge not quite vertical. The joint itself was found to be quite sound, the bolts and nuts being tight "and perfectly in position". Behind the joint flange, however, the inspecting officer found at the junction of web and the bottom flange, a large honeycomb, or draw-hole, which measured 3½ in. across the face. This hole was quite extensive. By filling it with water, the inspecting officer determined it had a capacity of 15½ in³, and, as the metal immediately around the hole was not sound, he considered the weakness was more extensive than the flaw appeared to indicate. At one place, the sectional area of the bottom flange had, he reckoned, been reduced by just under 25 per cent, "thus enormously decreasing the theoretical strength of the girder".

Major Marindin gave it as his opinion that part of this defect could have been seen in the maker's yard before the girder was painted. But, on the other hand which was really much more disturbing, afterwards, the flaw could not have been detected by the most minute inspection unless the girder had been taken to pieces. Quite obviously, the honeycomb or drawhole had been there when the casting was made; but the Major did not put all the blame on the founders. The engineer who designed the girder came in for his share of the criticism, and rightly so, too. "Such defects," ran the report, "are caused by the want of constant and careful feeding of the metal, it is an evidence of the want of the necessary precautions in the manufacture of this particular girder, which should have received more than ordinary attention on account of the objectionable pattern which was adopted by the engineer, and which, happily, is one never seen now in new bridges, and rarely in old ones." The central joint itself was said to be as strong as any other part of the girder, but it was nevertheless considered to be a distinct element of weakness because of the sharply varying thicknesses in the metal which gave rise to a far greater risk of imperfections during manufacture, than would be the case in a beam made all in one piece without the "stress-raising" changes in section occasioned by the bosses and vertical flanges needed for the joint.

Major Marindin could find no trace of evidence that a derailment had occurred either just before the train reached the bridge or after it had entered upon it. From what the engine crew said and from the position of the rolling stock after the accident, he was sure that the girder gave way suddenly as the engine was passing over it. Bearing in mind the requirement of the Board of Trade, namely that the breaking weight of the girder should be equal to six times the live load added to three times the dead load at the centre of the span, the bridge, assuming that the castings were sound, was up to strength in spite of there having been an increase of 5 tons in the weight of the engines using the line compared with those in vogue when the bridge had been new. Even so, in 1882, the heaviest engine working on the branch had a weight of only 21 tons 2 cwt 3 qtrs and 9⅓ lb. (If such accuracy of weight measurement could have been possible, it seems all the more remarkable that so little was known of the actual stresses in the girders in those days.)

> "Under the circumstances, [wrote the Major], I do not consider that any blame can be attached to the engineer of the Company or to his subordinates; but this conclusion, although in some respects satisfactory, is one which cannot but be the cause of perhaps more anxiety than if the failure of the girder could be attributed to want of supervision, or carelessness on the part of those responsible for the proper maintenance of the line; for if one such girder, which was of sufficient theoretical strength when cast, and which being in constant use for 25 years, had never shown any signs of weakness or outward flaw, suddenly breaks down, owing to a defect which must have existed when it was originally made, and had lasted ever since, it is very difficult to know what steps should be taken to guard against the recurrence of a like disaster."

Once more the unreliability of cast iron under tensile strain "especially when subjected to constant percussion" was brought to notice; and again little or nothing was done except to ban its use in bridges on lines built subsequently. On the G.N. of S.R., there were 91 underbridges of cast iron beams with spans of 25 ft or more, and of these, eight had girders of design similar to that which had failed at Inverythan.

The inspecting officers of the Board of Trade could only make recommendations. The law did not bind the various railway companies to any hard and fast ruling; if another cast iron girder bridge were to fail, the directors would not have been held to blame if it were proved that the said girders had been put into the line at some time previous to the issue of the recommendations. It was only when the calculated risk of the continued use of cast iron beam girders exceeded the cost of their replacement, that anything like the universal abandonment of all cast iron underbridges was likely to be carried out. So far the price of reconstruction seems to have kept ahead of that calculated risk. The number of cast iron beam girder underbridges in the British Rail system is getting smaller every year. That is true. But some of the reduction in numbers springs from the closing down of uneconomic lines.

CHAPTER 7

Trouble at Norwood Junction

THE compound cast iron girder trussed with wrought iron bars had gradually disappeared following the recommendations made at the 1847 Enquiry. After the Inverythan accident, the use of cast iron girders in any form other than arches, came to be prohibited for underline bridges on *new* lines after August 1883. Yet there continued to exist many hundreds of cast iron beam bridges, any one of which could have been a potential killer through the presence of hidden flaws. Familiarity did breed contempt; the safety of hundreds of small-span underline bridges was still being taken for granted although there was no way of being really sure of their strength.

The effect of recommendations could be most disturbing. The sudden issue of orders to reconstruct or strengthen dozens of bridges could be very upsetting to a railway timetable. The directors of most of the companies, mindful of commerce and dividends, boggled at such ideas. They deferred the issue of orders to rid the lines of all cast iron girders; they were content to let things slide. After all, they argued, a bridge which had stood for thirty years and showed no outward and visible sign of deterioration, seemed just as likely to be safe for another thirty years even if the weights of engines were on the increase.

Besides, the beam at Inverythan had been a two-casting affair with a thoroughly objectionable joint coming bang in the middle of the span just where bending strains were greatest. The beam made all in one casting was a different thing altogether; surely, it was above suspicion.

So when a cast iron girder in the Portland Road Bridge at Norwood Junction suddenly gave way under a crack express on 1 May 1891, the news came like a bolt from the blue. It was especially worrying because, fifteen years before, following a derailment in an adjacent siding on the very same bridge, the attention of the directors of the London Brighton & South Coast Railway Company had been drawn to a deficiency in the strength of the bridge. They had ignored entirely a recommendation made by the Board of Trade that stronger girders should have been substituted under the running lines. It was providential that the accident was not accompanied with any fatalities, otherwise the Chief Engineer and perhaps the directors as well might have found themselves facing charges of manslaughter. Actually, the company got off very lightly; the worst casualty among five passengers injured was a dislocated ankle though ninety others complained of a nasty shake up.

Major-General C. S. Hutchinson, R.E., reported on the accident. The train was the 8.45 a.m. from Brighton. Drawn by one of Stroudley's newest 0-4-2 engines (she had appeared in December 1890), No. 175 "Hayling", it consisted of a four-wheeled brake van, four six-wheeled first class carriages, two bogie "firsts", a bogie Pullman car "Jupiter", three bogie "firsts" and another four-wheeled brake van. Incidentally, one four-wheeled brake, a bogie "first" and a six-wheeled "first" with passengers for Victoria, had been slipped at East Croydon.

The speed was estimated to have been at least 40 miles an hour, and the derailment had taken place when the engine was on the bridge. Nevertheless, the whole train got across the bridge except for the rear brake van which ended up poised over Portland Road. All the carriages were derailed; all remained upright, and the train was brought to a standstill by the Westinghouse continuous brake within its own length.

The report on the accident is remarkably detailed, and it gives us today a very good picture of what conditions were like on a heavily-worked suburban line at the close of the nineteenth century; and some digression from our story of bridges alone is amply justified.

Every little item of damage has been listed and priced. The leading brake van with electric light apparatus for lighting the carriages was a write-off at £450. The engine and tender with two guard-irons broken, a sand-pipe and casting broken, horn-stay studs, brake-rods bent, the footplate damaged and the boiler leaking, was said to have sustained £50 worth of damage. Admittedly, the C.M.E.'s bill was not a high one, but one might be forgiven for wondering how the leaking boiler could be blamed on the accident! The Pullman car had the floor strained, platforms damaged, bogie-frames strained and broken, windows cracked and interior fittings damaged, costing £120 for repairs. There were, of course, other damages to the rest of the train, and the whole bill for repairing the rolling stock came to £1850.

The track, straight in the vicinity of the bridge, consisted of chaired permanent way with double-headed steel rails weighing 78 lb to the yard, and in lengths of 21 ft. It was about ten years old; and although the inspecting officer saw no reason to suppose the permanent way was in a bad state of repair, he thought it possible that there might have been some slackness in the rail joints on the bridge "whereby a greater strain than necessary may have been communicated to the girder".

The bridge was originally constructed by the London & Croydon Railway Company and it then had a span of 20 ft, the girders being cast iron trough-shaped beams. In 1859 and 1860, after it had become the property of the L.B. & S.C.R., the bridge had been reconstructed when Norwood Junction station was remodelled. The span was increased to 25 ft on the square or 26·75 ft measured on the skew. The bridge carried seven tracks, each carried on a 4-in. planking fastened to cross-girders resting on the bottom flanges of 27 in. deep cast iron main girders. There was no ballast on the bridge, the rail-chairs being spiked directly to the planking. Each main girder was 30 ft long and had ten sockets cast on one side for receiving the cross-girders, each of which consisted of two rails bolted together but separated by a shaped baulk of timber. The bottom flanges of the main girders were 20 in. wide with a thickness at the web of $1\frac{3}{4}$ in. and tapering to $1\frac{1}{2}$ in.; the web was off-centre, the flange projecting $13\frac{1}{4}$ in. on the inside where it carried the cross-girders.

The bridge had separate superstructures under each track. Under the Up Main, the left-hand beam broke into three pieces and fell into the roadway. Subsequent examination showed a flaw in the bottom flange which extended from within $\frac{1}{2}$ in. of the underside of the girder to a point 7 in. up the web. It was estimated that this flaw reduced the load-carrying capacity of the beam by at least one-fourth; but, even without the loss of strength caused by the flaw, these cast iron beams had what the inspecting officer described as a deficiency of strength of nearly 12 tons. Under the Board of Trade rules issued in 1859, each girder should have had a minimum breaking load of six times the moving load plus three times the dead load, amounting in this case to 82·98 tons. But the calculated load under which the beam should have been expected to fail, supposing the casting to be sound, was only 71 tons.

To make matters worse, the Stroudley 0-4-2 engine which drew the express and gave a moving load equivalent to 12·33 tons at the centre of each girder was by no means the heaviest locomotive regularly working trains over Portland Road Bridge. The South Eastern had engines giving a correspondingly equivalent loading of 12·6 tons, the Great Eastern 12·7 tons, and the London & NorthWestern 14·3 tons.

The cast iron girders had been delivered by the Horseley Iron Company on 7 February 1860. The flaw, though hidden after the beam had been erected, actually extended to the surface of the web; and it should have been spotted by the company's inspector before it left the works. The flaw, which was really a void or blow-hole in the cast iron, was found to be covered by a thin sheet of wrought iron used in the operation of casting the girder, and kept in position by a vertical piece of nail iron about ¼ in. square and 7 in. long.

Major-General Hutchinson, reporting that the Brighton Company "was deserving of much blame for having omitted to substitute stronger girders", appears to have let them off lightly for he continued: "It is satisfactory to be able to express the opinion that it was owing to the nature and strength of the vehicles composing the express train, and to the prompt application of the Westinghouse brake that so comparatively little personal injury or damage to rolling-stock was sustained."

Commenting on the accident in its issue of 8 May 1891, The Engineer summed up with these words: "No better material can be used than cast iron for small bridges where there is room, but it is not now used where it must carry heavy and suddenly-applied loads, which are supported by resistance to transverse stress."

No doubt, with so many cast iron underbridges in the line, it was necessary to avoid giving cause for alarm among the travelling public. Nevertheless, the Brighton Company lost no time in calling in Sir John Fowler to report on the state of not only all cast iron underbridges but also the Grosvenor Road Bridge over the Thames, Rastrick's Ouse Valley Viaduct, the Shoreham Bridge over the River Adur, and several others. Of 171 cast iron underbridges on the L.B. & S.C.R., 81 were to be reconstructed within 3 years, and the remainder were to follow as soon as possible. Other companies followed suit, and on the Midland Railway alone, 181 cast iron bridges were replaced at a cost of £85,000.

CHAPTER 8

Wrought Iron Girders

THE stories of the building of the Britannia Tubular Bridge across the Menai Straits by Robert Stephenson, and of the last great work of Isambard Kingdom Brunel over the Tamar at Saltash, have been told many times. But in none of the accounts to be found in the history books is there any reference to the importance of both these crossings in the development of the art of designing and making girderwork.

For both Stephenson and Brunel, the crossings presented a challenge to their ingenuity. For the first time, these engineers were up against the problems of bridging waterways in which it was not practicable to build temporary works on which to erect their permanent structures. The two men were friends, but at the same time they were professional rivals; neither intended to follow slavishly the other's practice, but each did his best to help the other. They were active members of the Institution of Civil Engineers, and during the meetings of that august body, Stephenson and Brunel had many discussions about each other's problems. In the closing years of their lives, each was in the running for election as President; Robert took office in the year 1855, Isambard as one of the Vice-Presidents would have held that distinguished post had it not been for his untimely death on 15 September 1859. The two had dined together on the previous Christmas Day at Shepheard's Hotel in Cairo.

Joseph Locke, M.P., the President of the Institution of Civil Engineers in that momentous year when Robert Stephenson and I. K. Brunel died, spoke at the first meeting at Great George Street held after the country had lost its two illustrious sons, and said: "We, at least, who are benefited by their successes, who feel that our Institution has reason to be proud of its association with such names as Brunel and Stephenson, have a duty to perform; and that duty is, to honour their memory and emulate their example."

So far as bridge-building is concerned, there is no doubt the world was only too ready to follow the practices in the art of building bridges with girders designed and made according to the principles laid down by Stephenson and Brunel and their assistants. The cases of the Britannia Tubular and the Royal Albert bridges are strangely similar; for the former, Stephenson had a trial run at Conway, and the crossing of the River Wye at Chepstow was to be Brunel's guinea-pig. Though the schemes of each of these two engineers were as different as chalk and cheese, both were to set the pattern upon which the shape of future girders was to be based. Stephenson was a year or two in advance of his rival, but Brunel with his "broad gauge" Great Western Railway was every bit a match for the exponents of the "narrow gauge" lines. The race was a dead heat so far as bridges were concerned.

At all previous river-crossings it had been possible to drive wooden piles into the river beds and put the permanent bridges together *in situ* on falsework which was taken away afterwards. Brunel had crossed the Thames with his first bow-and-string truss of 202 ft at Windsor (opened in 1849) in this way; the wrought ironwork made in Bristol was erected on scaffolding supported on piles driven into the bed of the river, and afterwards all the temporary work below the bridge was taken away. There was nothing special about that way of building a bridge; nearly every masonry arch had been put together, stone by stone, supported on falsework underneath. But at Conway and Chepstow, Stephenson and Brunel had to think along different lines; and, in so doing, they had to depart from the use of the then more conventional materials cast iron and timber, and turn their attention to riveted girders of wrought iron. Of course, Brunel never was in favour of using cast iron for beams if he could avoid it; Stephenson, as we have seen, was a little too complacent and he had been content to go on employing compound cast iron beams trussed with wrought iron bars for spans 100 ft long and over.

Stephenson was helped enormously by Fairbairn who had had valuable experience in constructing the wrought iron hulls of steamships. Brunel derived practical benefits from similar work on which he had

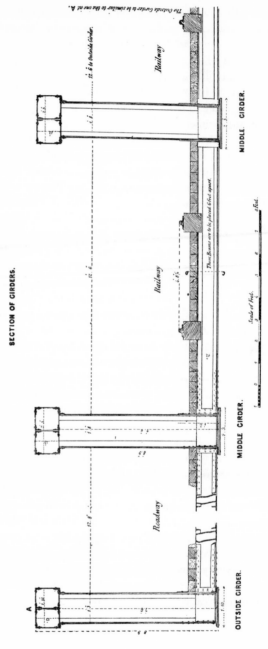

FIG. 7. Combined road and railway bridge of riveted wrought iron girders with hollow rectangular box-section compression flanges. The drawing of this particular bridge over the River Medlock on the ArdwickBranch Railway was shown at the 1847 Enquiry.

himself been engaged. Both men owed debts of gratitude to their fathers who were only slightly less famous as engineers; Stephenson had followed in the footsteps of his father who was perhaps best known for his mechanical skill and the "Rocket", winner of the Rainhill locomotive trials; Isambard Kingdom had been designing bridges and working on Marc Isambard Brunel's greatest work namely the Thames Tunnel. To Robert Stephenson, the bridge was incidental to the railways, whereas I. K. Brunel started to build the Great Western Railway *after* he had interested the Merchant Venturers in the design of a suspension bridge to cross the Clifton Gorge at Bristol. L. T. C. Rolt, in his book *George and Robert Stephenson, the Railway Revolution*, quotes F. R. Conder, an engineer who knew both our heroes:

> "The imperfections in the character of Mr Brunel [wrote Conder] were of the heroic order. He saw always clearly before him the *thing* to be done and the way to do it, although he might be deficient in the choice and the management of the human agency which was necessary to effect his designs. Mr Stephenson, on the other hand, knew how to derive from his staff and his friends a support and an aid that carried him, at times, over real engineering difficulties with a flowing sheet. It may be that the perfection and success of each individual work was more the study and aim of Mr Brunel, the return of benefit to the shareholders the more present idea to Mr Stephenson. The former preferred the luxurious cabins of Atlantic steamers and the commodious sofas of the Broad Gauge carriages; the latter opened the way for parliamentary and workmen's trains."

Robert Stephenson was confronted with the problem of bridging both the Menai Straits and the Conway estuary together in the same railway, namely the line from Chester to Holyhead for the Royal Mail route to Dublin. He was therefore scheming for both bridges at the same time. Brunel, on the other hand, was to bridge the Wye at Chepstow more than seven years before he came to the Tamar; the first of these two bridges was on the line to South Wales, the second was to join Cornwall on to England.

So, first of the four big bridges was Conway, a single 400-ft span of two wrought iron tubes, each of which weighed more than 1000 tons. Each tube was a rectangular box 18 ft 6 in. high and 14 ft wide, with nine plate girders on top, and seven underneath, forming box-like cellular compression and tension flanges. These cells were only 21 in. deep inside, and to anyone subject to claustrophobia, progress through the 400-ft long boxes must have been most unpleasant. The trains were, of course, to run through the 18-ft high box of each tube. The girder-work was fabricated by Messrs Garforth of Dukinfield near Manchester, taken in small pieces to a convenient site on the shore near the crossing, and built into the tubes which were in due course floated out on pontoons to their final resting places and then raised by jacks to the required level. At Conway, the headway below the bridge is not great, and the amount of jacking (about 12 ft) was quite small compared with what was to come later at the Menai Straits.

Stephenson appointed Edwin Clark as his resident engineer, first at Conway and later at the Britannia Tubular Bridge; and Brunel lent Captain Claxton, R.N., to assist over the navigation details involved in floating the awkward cumbersome tubes from the shore to the bridge sites. The arrangements at both bridges followed the same general pattern; but over the Straits, the two centre spans were each of 460 ft and the tubes weighed more than 1500 tons apiece. And after being landed, the Britannia tubes had to be lifted away up the high towering piers so as to afford the minimum clearance of 100 ft above high water which Their Lordships of the Admiralty had insisted upon; and once up, the tubes of the five-span Britannia Tubular Bridge were to be joined together so that eventually each tube became continuous throughout the full 1511 ft of the bridge.

Nevertheless, Conway was the guinea-pig, and although the piers and abutments of both bridges had been building simultaneously since the spring of 1846, the floating of the first of the Conway tubes in March 1847 actually heralded this method of erecting large girder bridges by prefabrication on shore and subsequently floating into position. This particular tube was conveyed across the water on six pontoons, and history tells us that Brunel, hands in pockets and cigar in mouth, stood alongside Robert Stephenson on the top of the tube while Captain Claxton newly back from seeing to the S.S. *Great Britain* ashore in Dundrum Bay, had charge of the arrangements for navigating the floating mass.

The middle pier of the Britannia Tubular Bridge towers 230 ft above the rock from which the bridge takes its name. It has been said that this great height above the tubes was part of the erection scheme and it housed the hydraulic gear for raising the tubes. This is only partly the explanation. Even after the construction of the piers had been taken in hand, Stephenson had apparently not made up his mind definitely that

the Straits could be spanned by plate girders alone. Professor Hodgkinson, leading technologist of the day, and a considerable band of eminent
scientists were saying it was foolish to attempt the bridge without provision for the use of suspension chains; and that accounts for the seem-
ingly unnecessary height of the piers and the "windows" near the top
through which the chains would have passed. At that early stage,
Stephenson was having to play safe; the experiments which Fairbairn
was to conduct on such extensive lines, had not yet been carried through.
Later, as we know, Stephenson wisely went ahead without the chains,
and the great tubular plate girder bridges across the water at Conway
and the Menai Straits bear testimony to his farsightedness. But Brunel,
the individualist, had his own ideas. No less ingenious, the Chepstow
and the Royal Albert Bridge were to employ the principles of the suspension bridge.

The Conway Bridge was strengthened in 1899 when the span length
of each tube was reduced by the addition of intermediate supports
given by cast iron cylinder piers sunk into the river bed at points about
50 ft in front of each abutment. This strengthening, which included
some heavy stiffening at the new points of support, is all that has been
necessary to keep Stephenson's girders abreast of modern loading
requirements. At the Menai Straits, the continuity resulting from joining the tubes together at each pier, had already provided a comparatively large margin of strength.

Abroad, Stephenson's bridgework did not go unnoticed. Canada
copied the same form of rectangular tubular girder construction for a
1¾ mile long bridge carrying the Grand Trunk Railway across the
St. Lawrence river at Montreal. The superstructure of this remarkable
bridge was in fact designed by Robert Stephenson. Construction
started in 1853; and after being opened by H.R.H. the Prince of Wales
in 1860 and named the Victoria Bridge, it was acclaimed the "Eighth
Wonder of the World". The total length of the tubes was 6592 ft and
their weight was 9044 tons. They lasted until 1898 by which time
the railway had had more than enough of the smoke nuisance in the
tunnel-like structure.

In India, similar tubular girder construction was, at one time,
favoured for a bridge to carry the Grand Trunk Road and the North
Western Railway across the River Indus at Attock. The site was close
to tribal country on the North-West frontier, and the solid plate girder

walls of such a bridge appealed to the military authorities because of the cover they would have afforded from snipers' bullets. But other ideas prevailed; after a half-hearted attempt to tunnel under the Indus, the crossing was finally made with a fine double-deck truss bridge designed by Sir Guilford Molesworth (compiler of the well-known engineers' pocket-book) and opened in 1883.

PLATE 5. Rastrick's road bridge of 1816 across the River Wye at Chepstow still carries the traffic using the A48 route from Gloucester to South Wales though steel ribs now strengthen the cast iron arches. (Photo: B.R.)

PLATE 6. At Conway, the 400-ft span of the 1847 tubes was reduced when the intermediate piers were added to strengthen the bridge in 1899.

PLATE 7. The balloon flange of a wrought iron girder of 1848 cut open during the reconstruction of Over Junction Bridge across the River Severn at Gloucester. (Photo: B.R.)

PLATE 8. Robert Stephenson designed tall piers with windows to accommodate suspension chains at the Britannia Tubular Bridge.

PLATE 9. A Down goods rumbles across Brunel's 1852 truss span at Chepstow Bridge.

PLATE 10. Stroudley's 0-4-2 "Gladstone" of the same class as "Hayling", derailed when the Portland Road Bridge gave way at Norwood Junction on 1 May 1891. (Photo: Locomotive Pub. Co.)

PLATE II. At Chepstow giant-size wedges kept the A-frame struts pressing hard down on the suspension chains; rollers in an oil-bath gave limited movement horizontally. (Photo: B.R.)

PLATE 12. Inside one of the tubes at Saltash, an engineer uses a pendulum to study movement in the giant strut as a train crosses the Royal Albert Bridge. (Photo: B.R.)

PLATE 13. Jacking the saddle down against the suspension chains to restore the correct force in the upstream vertical of the Devon span truss of the Royal Albert Bridge. (Photo: B.R.)

PLATE 14. The completed joint on the Royal Albert Bridge as modified
in 1960. (Photo: B.R.)

CHAPTER 9

I. K. Brunel and the Chepstow Bridge

A CIVIL engineer has been defined as one who does for one dollar the work which the ordinary mortal accomplishes for two dollars. Both Stephenson and Brunel were civil engineers, and we have read Conder's description of their characters. If Brunel did put the solution of engineering problems first, and did perhaps tend to overlook his duty to the shareholders of the Great Western Railway, there is not the slightest doubt that Brunel was the better engineer when it came to the art of bridging.

In making comparison between Robert Stephenson bridging at Conway with Brunel taking the railway across the Wye at Chepstow, we must be fair to both. The Conway Bridge was opened for a single-line of "narrow-gauge" railway in April 1848, which was more than four years earlier than the first line of "broad-gauge" at Chepstow. So Stephenson might be said to have had the greater amount of pioneering to do; throughout the time the Conway and the Britannia Tubular bridges were on the drawing-board, he was being pestered by the directors of the Chester & Holyhead Railway anxious to see some return on the £1 million invested in their line. In fact the piers and abutments of both bridges were going ahead well before the details of the superstructures had been finalized. Studying Edwin Clark's two volumes describing both bridges, one cannot help noticing the continual submission of ideas about the bridges and the mode of their erection, to Stephenson by Fairbairn, Clark himself and many others. And, as often the replies contained excuses for delay caused by other business in the Houses of Parliament and elsewhere, the impression is gained that Stephenson was too far removed from the projects, and that too much had to be entrusted to assistants who though competent were unable to make important decisions without the approval first of Stephenson himself.

The story at Chepstow was so very different. The evidence of the master-mind was to be found in every detail meticulously worked out in the Duke Street office in London. I. K. Brunel had been present at Conway and the Menai Straits when the tubes had been floated out and although he never openly criticized the work of his professional colleague, he was profoundly shocked at the number of setbacks to progress at both the tubular bridges. Cast iron lifting beams and frames had cracked; hydraulic cylinders had proved to be spongy and leaking. Nothing seemed to have been properly worked out beforehand; indeed, from the very inception of both bridges when the substructure work had been planned to accommodate suspension chains in case they were wanted either for erection purposes or for permanent additions to the tubular spans, Conway and the Britannia bridges had been proceeded with on the assumption that all difficulties would be dealt with as they were met. In other words, there was virtually no proper forward planning. The results were to be reflected in the high costs.

Admittedly, a span length exceeding 400 ft was quite extraordinary for a railway bridge at that time; but at neither bridge did Stephenson have to contend with any difficult under-water foundation works. Conway Bridge cost £145,190 18s. 0d. and it was opened to the double-line of 4 ft 8½ in. gauge railway on 16 December 1848. It took the lines across an opening 400 ft wide.

At Chepstow, less than four years later, Brunel took the two tracks of the 7 ft gauge South Wales Railway across a gap of 600 ft over the River Wye, for an all-in cost of only £77,000; and he was faced with having to sink the foundations far below water level in a river which had the second highest tidal range in the world.

Brunel had used timber-trussed spans to carry the railway over the River Usk at Newport and across a deep and wide valley at Landore near Swansea; and his first thoughts for bridging the Wye had been to use timber-trussed arches. But the Lords of the Admiralty had stepped in and insisted upon a bridge having a level soffit giving an uninterrupted head-room of 50 ft above high water over a width of 300 ft. This was because in those days sailing ships used to come right up the Wye almost

as far as Rastrick's cast iron arch road bridge; and although the site of
the railway bridge was less than half a mile downstream from the road
bridge, ocean-going craft had to be given facilities for berthing opposite the Customs' house which had been located conveniently near to
the highway.

The site of the railway bridge is remarkable for the contrasts between
the two banks of the river. On the Gloucestershire side, the river flows
against the foot of a limestone cliff 120 ft high on the left bank; whereas, on the Monmouthshire side, the land behind the right bank is of low-
lying sedimentary deposits inundated whenever heavy rainfall in the
Welsh borderlands coincides with high spring tides.

Brunel decided to bridge the opening with two 300-ft lengths of his
"standard" form of half-through type wrought iron plate girderwork
for each line of railway. Over the navigable channel, he supported the
300-ft length of girders from "suspension" chains above; over the
shallow water and on to the right bank of the river, he built conventional piers to support the girders from below. Coming from Gloucester, the railway was in a cutting and it emerged quite suddenly on
to the bridge which started 50 ft above the river and well up the cliff
face; once across the bridge, the line continued on a high embankment
behind a massive stone abutment. All the piers of the bridge were to be
of cast iron cylinders filled with lime concrete.

Brunel was of course familiar with the experiments on tubular forms
carried out by Hodgkinson and Fairbairn; but, Brunel was never one
to follow fashion for fashion's sake. Individualist and engineer, he
preferred to do the thinking for himself. Stephenson's tubular girders
had proved excessively heavy for spans of 400 ft; for the shorter 300-ft
opening, such a design made deep enough to contain the train, could
have been even more wasteful. Nevertheless, the tube was ideal as a
strut to carry the forces of compression, and Brunel already well versed
in the construction of the hulls of ships made up of riveted wrought
iron plates, was quick to realize that a circular form of tube would be
very much more appropriate provided the weight of the tube itself
could be taken care of by some kind of truss. Moreover, such a tube
would weigh but a fraction of the great rectangular boxes used at
Conway, and in consequence, would be very much easier to handle,
float and raise through upwards of a hundred feet.

Here was the real engineer at work, designing the bridge to suit the

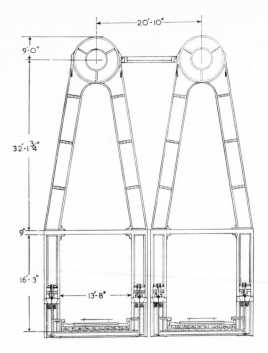

FIG. 8. Cross-section through Brunel's "river" spans at Chepstow.

site and the best way of getting it into position. The tube would hold apart the ends of "suspension" chains which would look after the tensile forces in a truss carrying the plate girder railway bridge below. Moreover, Brunel argued that the tube would be stiff, and with the railway deck "strutted" and "trussed" to the tube, the excessive distortions to which a suspension bridge is liable under the passage of a concentrated heavy load (such as a locomotive) would be avoided.

The Chepstow Bridge as Brunel built it became known as the Tubular Bridge. That was the name on local picture post cards of it, and on the colourful pictures which passengers on the Great Western Railway used to gaze upon when they were not looking out of the windows of their compartments. Each 300-ft span (there were separate superstructures for the Up and Down lines), depended upon a 9-ft tube of riveted wrought iron plates, to resist the inwards drag of the chains.

In that respect, the name was no misnomer; but, to the public familiar with Stephenson's tubular bridges which carried the trains in the darkness of the inside of the tubes, the description applied to Brunel's masterpiece was apt to be misleading.

At Conway, a tube had weighed upwards of 1000 tons when it was being floated, but once it had been landed on the abutments, that great weight had to be raised through a mere 12 ft. At Chepstow, Brunel was of course dealing with spans 100 ft shorter; but, with his tubes built on the flat land behind the shore of the right bank of the river, they had to be raised through more than 100 ft. And what was even more exacting, they had to be lifted clear of shipping within 12 hours. Besides, the near-vertical face of the limestone cliff did not lend itself to simple hydraulic jacking arrangements. So Brunel wisely kept the weight of the prefabricated parts, i.e. the tubes, as low as possible.

The tubes at Chepstow, 9 ft in diameter and 312 ft long, weighed a mere 138 tons apiece. But they were not self-supporting. Without the inward pull from the chains at each end, and the upward support of the posts or struts of the "trusses", the tubes could not be expected to carry their own dead weight. This fact was to present a problem to the engineers who took the tubes down in 1962.

So Brunel trussed each tube with temporary chains borrowed from the permanent diagonal bracing of each span, and he entrusted the whole of the raising to block and tackle with chains passing over pulleys held aloft on temporary timber trestling. And he built each tube with an upward camber of 30 in. at the middle of its length.

The tube for the Down line was the first to be put together and Brunel had it trussed with its permanent chains and set up for testing before he allowed it to be launched. Of course, that was a temporary expedient, and the 50-ft deep trusswork was all taken away before the actual flotation of the tube took place.

The tube was built on the low ground upstream of the site of the railway bridge and parallel with the bank of the river. With his customary insistence on proper preparations beforehand, Brunel had detailed drawings made showing exactly how the tube was to be manoeuvred into its launching position at right angles to the river bank and underneath where the "land" spans were to be. Once the tube had been brought round and it lay between the cast iron pillars of the pier and with its nose overhanging the timber staging, it was a simple matter to

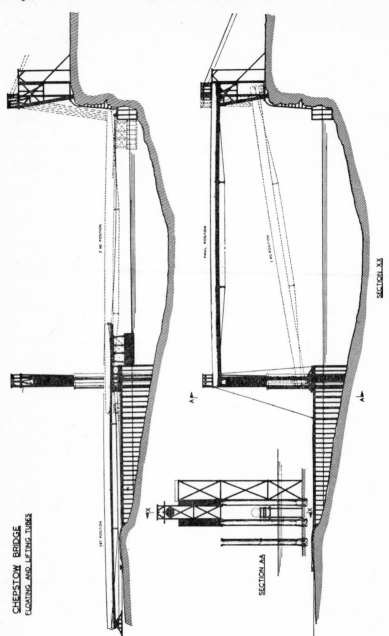

CHEPSTOW BRIDGE
FLOATING AND LIFTING TUBES

1ST POSITION

2 ND POSITION

FINAL POSITION

1 RD POSITION

SECTION XX

SECTION AA

FIG. 1. Page 62, method of erecting the 300 ft. long tubes used in the "girder" spans at Chepstow.

bring a pontoon of six barges under the end of the tube. Then, with the tail end suitably mobile on a carriage mounted on a temporary railway track, the tube was launched end-on across the river.

On Thursday, 8 April 1852, the launching started a little after 9 o'clock in the morning, and by a quarter to ten the pontoon had reached the far bank when "without any delay the chains of the lifting tackles were attached". Certainly there would have been no time to lose because there is a rise and fall of more than 40 ft in the tidal estuary of the Wye and slack water at high tide lasts only a few minutes.

We are told that all proceeded with "perfect quiet and regularity under the management of Mr Brunel who was assisted by Mr Brereton and Captain Claxton". And the tube was duly lifted in the course of the day to the level of the railway where it was, of course, well clear of the masts of ships. Very shortly afterwards, the tube reached the tops of the towers and was duly set on its bearings; expansion roller-bearings on the masonry portal-tower on the cliff and "fixed" bearings on the top of the "river" tower which was built of bolted cast iron work above the cylinders of the pier.

The choice of the positioning of the roller-bearings on the abutment tower has always struck the writer as being rather odd because that portal tower was much more massive than the rather light cast iron-work of the "river" tower, and it was therefore much better fitted to withstand the forces set up by the traction and braking of trains which must necessarily be transmitted through the rigid "fixed" bearings. Perhaps Brunel reasoned that the rock strata on the cliff face should not be subjected to any horizontal forces. When, in 1962, the bridge was reconstructed, the expansion bearings under the 300-ft spans were, like those under Brunel's tubes, located on the cliff abutment.

It is of interest to note that the cast ironwork for the portal tower came from the Irish Engineering Co. and was made at the Seville Iron-works in Dublin. This too might seem curious because in the map which accompanied the Report issued on conclusion of the 1847 Enquiry and purported to show the location of all reputable iron foundries in the British Isles, there is no indication that any existed in Ireland. Brunel had, however, had reason to visit Dublin when his precious iron steamship the *Great Britain* went ashore in Dundrum Bay in 1846. She had left Liverpool on 22 September for New York, and after she had been ashore for some weeks, Brunel, who had decided she was not seriously damaged, took steps to protect her from the winter gales with a vast mattress of strong fagots.

The then finest ship in the world as Brunel described the S.S. *Great Britain*, was duly saved through her designer's efforts; and it may well be that in his journeyings to County Down, Brunel had been favourably impressed by the capabilities of the foundry in Dublin. In any case, the demand for cast iron in 1848 was exceeding the capacities of most of the foundries in Britain, and the facilities for delivery by sea from Dublin to Chepstow would have been an additional attraction.

To return to the erection of the 300-ft spans of the Chepstow Bridge, history glosses over the fitting of the permanent trusses and we learn that the Down line spans were opened to single-line traffic on 14 July 1852. The Up line spans were completed in the following April. Was Bastille Day of any especial significance to Brunel? Perhaps. For his ancestors had farmed in Normandy and his father had been a fugitive when he escaped from Paris in January 1836. Isambard displayed a remarkable sense of humour; at one time, he slung a rope and pulley across a busy London thoroughfare so that he and his friend across the road could exchange notes between their upstairs windows; and on another occasion when irritated by obstructive landowners, he had threatened to cut the turf from the chalky downs in Wiltshire so as to depict the engines of his broad gauge railway alongside the famous white horses. So, it is not beyond the realms of possibility that an impish mind should have chosen a date made famous in history, as the opening day for the first half of Chepstow Bridge. Whether the choice was really intentional or not, we shall never know; but, what we do know is that it was pure coincidence that Bastille Day 1962 saw the last Up train across the span on the Up line before reconstruction commenced to sweep away the second of Brunel's historic trusses.

Details of construction and, in particular, of the connections between the "suspension" chains and the plate girders, are worthy of attention. They demonstrate the ingenuity of the designer and the skill—one is almost tempted to say patience—of the platers and riveters of those days. The vertical struts bearing down on the chains and preventing the tubes from sagging were riveted rigidly to both the tubes and the plate girderwork which carried the railway track, but where these struts made contact with the chains, Brunel had introduced nests of iron rollers to give freedom of movement of the girderwork on the chains;

and because the chains inclined outwards from the pin connections at each end of the 9-ft diameter tubes to the line of the plate girders which were necessarily set about 15 feet apart since the trains had to run between them, Brunel cunningly introduced gun-metal rubbing strips to further reduce friction between the chains and the lower parts of the structure. The chains also gave support to the plate girders, which, as we have seen, were continuous throughout the span length of 300 ft, at two intermediate points in the middle portion between the struts. These supports were in the form of large screws and Brunel used them to adjust the tension in the chains. The chains were each formed of batches of links, alternating with 12 and 14 links 10 in. deep and varying in thickness from $\frac{11}{16}$ in. to $\frac{3}{4}$ in. Brunel went to great trouble to get links of lengths of 20 ft rolled in a single piece without welding on the eyes. "He had to go down himself to the manufactory in order to get the men into the way of doing the work."

But alas, brilliant as the design was, flexibility of the "suspension" truss under the passage of trains did in effect constitute a fundamental weakness in the structure. As a train entered upon a span, the plate girders naturally deflected between the abutment bearings and the first strut. This reduced the load pressing down on the knuckle pin screws ahead of the strut and in the middle part of the truss, and caused the shape of the chains to change with the result that the two struts, which were riveted to the tube above, were bent about their rigid connections. The secondary stresses caused by the deforming of the truss were quite alarmingly high: and after one of the plate girders in the "land" spans had partially collapsed in 1944, serious concern was felt for the future life of the big span over the water. And for many years the speed of all trains crossing the Chepstow Bridge was restricted to not more than 15 miles an hour.

CHAPTER 10

The Royal Albert Bridge

In describing the erection of the "tubular" spans of Brunel's bridge over the Wye at Chepstow, the accounts are surprisingly silent about the building of the "trusses" after the tubes had been got into place. Nevertheless, slinging the heavy chains and building the plate girders that carried the railway tracks below the circular tubes must have been difficult if not hazardous. Those who had the job of destressing the chains and "giggling" down the tubes in 1962, had the newly erected spans to work on; theirs was a simple job compared with the problem that confronted the erectors 110 years before.

When Brunel came to build his single-line railway bridge across the Tamar at Saltash, he prefabricated the trusses and the plate girder bridging slung below, on the shore before each 455-ft span was floated out and raised into position. In this, Brunel was emulating Stephenson who had prefabricated his rectangular tubes for the Conway and Menai Straits bridges. Today, it is still the endeavour of every bridge engineer to devise ways and means by which assembly aloft can be kept to a minimum; with labour and handling charges higher on site than in the confines of a workshop, it is the logical thing to do; but, as we shall see from the building of the Forth Bridge where 51,000 tons of steelwork was fashioned on site, it has not always been so. It was not until after 1948 when fabrication by welding instead of riveting was adopted, that the design of the steel girder bridge improved sufficiently to allow the whole of the fabrication of bridges for British Railways to be completed in the makers' works. Probably, Sir Gilbert Roberts's Severn Road Bridge, opened in 1966, is the finest example to date of what can be achieved through designing for complete prefabrication. There, 60 ft of completed bridge hoisted aloft in a matter of minutes, contrasted sharply with conditions at the Forth Road Bridge where only two years before it had taken weeks to erect a similar length of decking.

But to return to Saltash. Brunel had been scheming to bridge the Tamar since the Cornwall Railway Act had received the Royal Assent in 1846. Chepstow Bridge was opened in 1852; the Royal Albert came seven years later. So while he had been busy with the Wye trusses, Brunel must have been thinking over ideas for the bigger bridge.

The plans for the Royal Albert Bridge as we know it today finally got under way by the light of the gas-jets in Brunel's office at 18 Duke Street, Westminster, in the year after Chepstow had been opened. Again, Brunel used a combination of suspension chains and tubes for the trusses. But this time he gave the tubes as great a rise as the chains had droop at the middle of the span. He slung the familiar plate girder "bridging" that carries the railway track, below the trusses and hung it from eleven verticals which passed through the chains and extended right away up to the tubes, and from intermediate hangers located midway between the verticals and attached solely to the chains. So, in a way, the two great spans at Saltash are in fact fashioned on the principle of the suspension bridge. As such, they are unique in the world today. They are the only surviving suspension bridge spans carrying main line trains.

The design shows that Brunel was by no means unmindful of the shortcomings of the suspension bridge. To restrain the verticals and to counteract the tendency for them to be displaced longitudinally as the shape of the chains changed under the effect of a train moving across the bridge, he provided a continuous system of diagonal bracing. This bracing consisted of long wrought iron bars like the diagonal chains at Chepstow and tightened by wedges and cotters. Each end of the Saltash diagonals ended in a pin connecting it to the main truss work; and one curious thing about these connections is that the pins were intentionally made of a diameter $\frac{1}{8}$ in. less than the holes in which they took a bearing. We know that Brunel was very much preoccupied with other things at the time and his health was failing. So perhaps this extraordinary lapse from good practice may be accounted for by Brunel's absence elsewhere; but the fact remains that a pin bearing on a tiny area in a hole instead of all over is bound to work loose in a short time. Those whose duties have been to look after the Royal Albert Bridge had have good reason to regret this little fault in an otherwise remarkably fine structure.

The wrought iron riveted tubes at Saltash are elliptical in cross-section. They are 16 ft 9 in. broad and 12 ft 3 in. in height. So this time the chains hang in a vertical plane; one great improvement on the Chepstow design. The trusses have a depth of 56 ft at mid-span, and the tubes of the two spans are united over the centre pier where the bearings are fixed.

Each chain consists of two tiers of links, each tier being formed of 14 or 15 links, 7 in. deep and an inch thick. Part of these chains in Brunel's last great work came from Clifton where in 1831 after crossing swords with Thomas Telford he had scored his first success by winning a competition with his design for a bridge to span the famous Avon Gorge. In 1853, a shortage of funds for building the Clifton Suspension Bridge had lead to the sale of the chains, and Brunel had assisted by arranging to purchase the valuable wrought iron for use in the Cornwall Railway Company's project at Saltash. Eventually, the Clifton bridge, with the design suitably modified to accommodate the use of lighter and therefore weaker chains, was completed in 1864. The chains used at Clifton came from the Hungerford Bridge over the Thames which Brunel had built between 1841 and 1845, and which was taken down to make way for the Charing Cross railway bridge.

But to return to Saltash. The balance of the chains was supplied by Howard, Ravenhill & Co., of the King and Queen Iron Works at Rotherhithe. As at Chepstow, the links were made complete with the enlarged ends, all in one piece and without welding. A study of the links in these chains shows that at one end of each link, the outside edge of the eye has a smooth rounded curve while at the other end, the edge has definite shoulders. The latter are right-angled projections and their purpose was to provide a grip against which tackle could be attached when the heavy links were being bundled together and coupled up into a chain. Technically, they are referred to as clamping cheeks. Robert Stephenson had used clamping cheeks on the links of the chains used for raising the tubes at the Britannia Tubular Bridge; and, according to Edwin Clark, they were first thought of by Tierney Clark, designer of the neat little suspension bridge across the Thames at Marlow, who had adopted the idea in the links of the chains used in his well-known bridge over the Danube at Pesth.

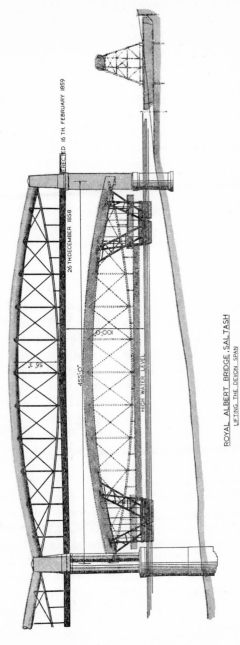

ROYAL ALBERT BRIDGE · SALTASH
LIFTING THE DEVON SPAN

ERECTED 16 TH FEBRUARY 1859

26 TH DECEMBER 1858

56' 3"

100'·0"

455'·0"

HIGH WATER LEVEL

FIG. 10. The method Brunel used to erect the prefabricated truss spans for the Royal Albert Bridge at Saltash.

The difficult operations of floating and lifting the spans at Saltash were carried out entirely by direct labour employed under Brunel and his assistants, there being no contractor engaged in or responsible for the work. Each truss was put together on the Devon shore and was assembled on timber falsework built parallel with and just off the land. The Cornish truss was the first to be completed. After it had been assembled, the ground near to the ends was dredged away from underneath it and two iron pontoons were floated into place under the truss. These pontoons carried an elaborate framework of timber, some of the principals used as props exceeding 40 ft in length.

Brunel directed the first floating personally, and 1 September 1857, the date chosen, was a beautiful quiet day without any wind.

Stephenson had lifted the tubes at Conway and the Britannia Tubular bridges by means of hydraulic presses "climbing" up chains on which the tubes were slung from cross-beams on the towers above. But at Saltash, Brunel put the hydraulic jacks underneath the spans, and built up the piers as the superstructure went up. And to simplify this operation, he temporarily accommodated the end lengths of the plate girders at a higher level and shunted them a little way along towards the middle of the span. This also enabled him to bring in the pontoons at a slightly higher level and meant that the truss did not have to be quite so high above the water while it was being floated out. The total weight of wrought ironwork in each span as floated out was 1060 tons or just over two-thirds of the weight of Stephenson's plate girder boxes of the Britannia Tubular Bridge which were only 11 ft longer.

At Saltash, the trusses were floated out on a rising tide, and thanks to the painstaking care with which the warping details had been worked out beforehand, each was landed on the following ebb. The trusses had to be raised through 87 ft, and this operation took eight months in the case of the Cornish span and five months in the case of the Devon span.

The Royal Albert Bridge was formally opened by H.R.H. the Prince Consort on 2 May 1859. It had been tested in the presence of Her Majesty's Chief Inspecting Officer of Railways, Colonel Yolland, the month before. Under a uniformly distributed test load amounting to 2·75 tons for every foot length of the trailway track, the Cornish span had deflected 7¾ in. and the Devon one 7½ in. In his report, Colonel Yolland wrote: "I regard these results as highly satisfactory, and so far as my knowledge goes, I believe them to be greatly superior to anything of the kind which has been attained elsewhere, and accomplished at less expenditure of money and materials." The greatest strain under the then normal train loading equivalent to about one ton per foot run, he estimated at $4 \cdot 2$ tons/in^2 of section in the wrought iron work.

The Royal Albert Bridge has a length of 2200 ft. In addition to the two 455-ft spans, there are seventeen half-through type plate girder spans ranging in length between 69 ft 6 in. and 93 ft. Isambard Kingdom Brunel died on 15 September 1859, less than six months after the Prince had opened his last great masterpiece, and the Directors of the Cornwall Railway in their subsequent half-yearly report to the shareholders, wrote:

> "Since the last half-yearly meeting you have lost the services of your celebrated engineer Mr Isambard Kingdom Brunel, whose works of extraordinary genius had earned for him a European reputation, and whose death will be a loss, not only to the Company, but to the general interests of science throughout the world. It is an act of justice to the memory of Mr Brunel, to place on record that the whole cost of the erection of that stupendous and beautiful structure, the Royal Albert Bridge, which has elicited the admiration of the whole scientific world, has not exceeded the sum of £225,000.
>
> "Considering the extraordinary difficulties which were overcome and the magnitude of the operation, it is believed that there is no engineering work in existence which has been more economically completed."

The Directors could have been more explicit. The sum of £225,000 covered not only the erection but the entire cost of the structure including the difficult work of founding the centre pier on rock at a depth of more than 87 ft below high water. Surely, no greater proof was needed of the ability of Brunel as an engineer; F. R. Conder (Chapter 8) had been proved wrong. Twice the sum spent on the single-line Royal Albert Bridge would not have met the bill of £601,865 for the double-track Britannia Tubular Bridge which not only carried the lighter loading of Stephenson's narrower gauge but was also shorter by over 600 ft.

The trusses at Saltash remain today virtually as Brunel built them, with the exception of the addition of a longitudinal horizontal bracing system halfway up the verticals and substantially stronger sway-bracing joining the up- and down-stream verticals above the railway track. Also, the timber decking under the ballasted permanent way which was altered to the standard 4 ft 8½ in. gauge in May 1892, has been strengthened by the duplication of the cross-girders; and all the approach spans were renewed in 1928–9.

There are, however, certain parts of the wrought ironwork on the Royal Albert Bridge which are quite inaccessible for painting and proper maintenance. The hanger plates below the middle verticals are a case in point. Short and inaccessible where they passed between the links of the chains, these plates failed through the effects of corrosion-fatigue. With the diagonals more or less out of action, the longitudinal displacement of the suspension chains caused by the movement of train loads across the bridge was being almost entirely resisted by these hangers; and, since the plate girders to which they were connected did not move longitudinally, the excessive slogging to and fro to which those hangers were subjected was something they could not endure indefinitely. Breakages occurred during the Second World War; temporary remedial measures in the shape of substantial straps enveloping the chains sufficed to keep the bridge in service; and the matter was finally attended to in 1960 when the connections were altered altogether. In the new arrangement, the plate girders are suspended from the verticals by pin-jointed hangers placed outside the chains where they can be easily got at for painting. At the same time, the bottom six feet of the centre verticals have been cut away and replaced with new parts of mild steel incorporating saddle-plates which were forced down on to the chains by hydraulic jacks while the new work was being fastened to the old wrought iron with high strength bolts. The improvements also included the renewal of the bottom parts of the adjoining diagonal bars; and these were duly tensioned by means of a screw-levering device which held these important bracings taut while the joints were being completed with high strength friction grip bolts.

Subsequently, all the diagonals were similarly tightened. But, as was to be expected, it has been impossible to prevent that change in the curvature of the chains which takes place whenever a load moves across a suspension bridge. However, lubrication and phosphor–bronze liners in the new hangers make due provision for all the movement likely to take place between the centre nodal points of the trusses and the plate girders on these unique suspension bridge spans.

The speed of trains crossing the Royal Albert Bridge has never been high because of the need to pick up by hand the tablet on entering the single-line section. But, apart from this, speed has been and still is

ROYAL ALBERT BRIDGE

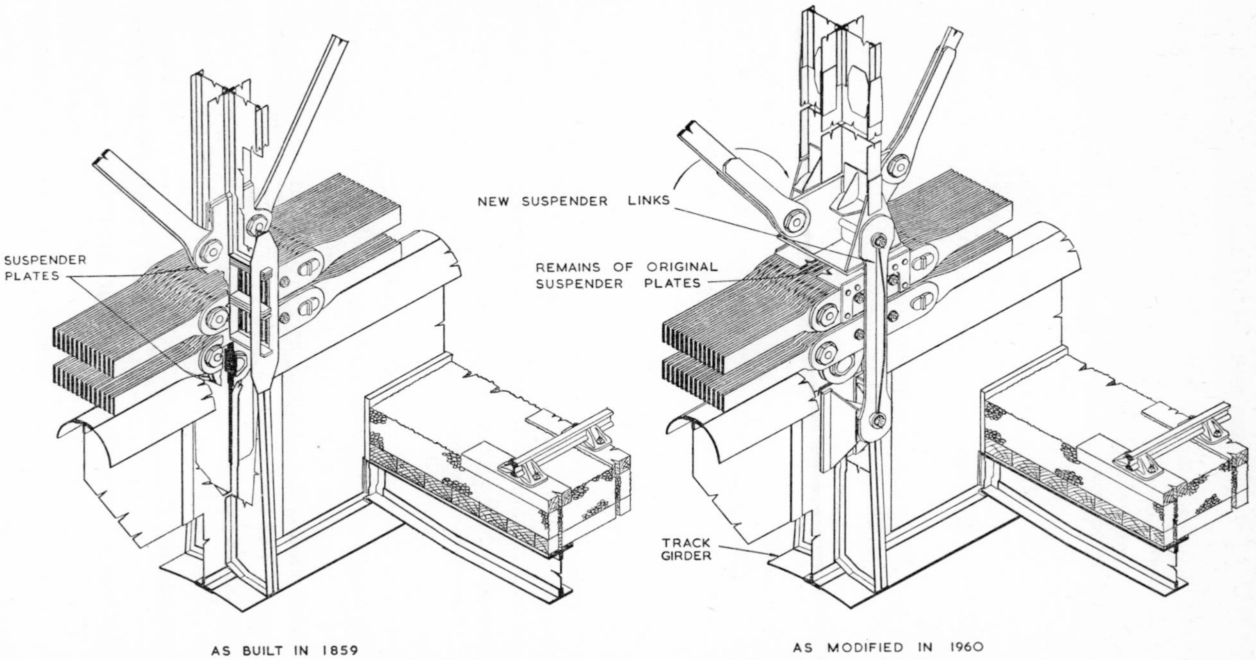

NEW SUSPENDER LINKS

REMAINS OF ORIGINAL SUSPENDER PLATES

SUSPENDER PLATES

TRACK GIRDER

AS BUILT IN 1859

AS MODIFIED IN 1960

SUSPENDERS AT CENTRES OF TRUSS SPANS

FIG. 11. The alterations to the suspenders at the centres of the truss spans at Saltash.

restricted to not more than 15 miles an hour on account of the sharp curves on the approaches. However, the Royal Albert is not a weak bridge. It is stronger today than it was when it was opened. So far as the strength of the girderwork is concerned, the heaviest locomotives could have been permitted to work trains across if it had been desired to do so. It was not the Royal Albert that kept the "King" class engines out of Cornwall. In February 1967, china clay trains from Burngullow to Sittingbourne in Kent were imposing axle-loadings of 22½ tons on the bridge.

Nevertheless, the distortion of the curvature of the chains—the lower chords of the "trusses"—remained a source of weakness; and in 1968, when trains of 100-ton bogie wagons were introduced to transport china clay refuse out of Cornwall as a building material, another attempt was made to "steady" the chains by bracing them with steel diagonals fastened to the plate girders of the track-carrying structure.

The future life of any bridge depends upon how well the fabric can be looked after. Brunel tended to pay more attention to the appearance of his bridges than to the facilities for painting the ironwork. He tidied up the ends of girders by masking them with masonry, cast iron, etc; and, in so doing, he hid important bearings from view; he left room for the rain to drive in, but no space for a paint brush. The Royal Albert was no exception. Where the plate girders entered the piers, where the hangers passed through the chains, where the chains entered the tubes, and where the verticals came up against the rounded surface of the tubes, he left problems well-nigh impossible of solution. At all these inaccessible places, the iron is vulnerable to the ravages of corrosion. Maintenance is costing £80,000 spread over four years, and including the strengthening to carry the 25-ton axle loads of the 100-ton bogie wagons. But this is a small price to pay for the upkeep of this fine old bridge. The cost of a new railway crossing would run into millions of pounds. The Tamar Road Bridge, that locked-coil cable suspension bridge with its graceful 1100-ft span less than 200 ft north of the railway, opened in April 1962, cost £1·84 million. An annual expenditure of £20,000 is, after all, less than a tenth of the cost of keeping the Severn Tunnel dry enough for that rail link with South Wales to be kept open.

Like all ageing structures, the Royal Albert Bridge will, so long as trains run west of Plymouth, continue to exercise to an ever increasing extent the ingenuity and patience of those engineers who are entrusted with the preservation of this monument to Isambard Kingdom Brunel. Reminded of the genius of one of the world's greatest engineering pioneers, they have good reason to be proud of their job. In their care is a historic structure which is surely a part of our national heritage.

CHAPTER 11

Arrol and the Superlatives

No one man ever built a bridge. But there have been men who, by making some major contribution to the art of bridge-building, have played an outstanding part in advancing the science and industry of structural engineering. The names of Thomas Telford, George and Robert Stephenson, and the Brunels, father and son, come to mind. However, famous as were these pioneers in the field of bridge construction, none did more to further and improve the reputation of the British steelwork industry than William Arrol, builder of the Forth Bridge, the world's mightiest railway bridge of all time.

William Arrol was born in the Renfrewshire village of Houston on 13 February 1839. Like all truly great men, he had a character in which firm determination and an ability to make decisions and keep them, was tempered with an overriding sense of kindness and consideration for others. Although he had started from the lowly position of blacksmith's apprentice and was to become one of the most famous of all bridge-builders, Arrol never forgot his friends on the shop-floor, the men by whose labours the name of his firm, Sir William Arrol & Co., Ltd., of Bridgeton, Glasgow, was, years later, to be connected with the building of the greatest road bridges across the estuaries of the Forth and the Severn.

Arrol died on 20 February 1913 and he was buried in Woodside cemetery in Paisley. More than ten years after his death in harness a week after his seventy-fourth birthday, journeymen fitters and platers and other workers in the machine shops at Dalmarnock Iron Works still boasted of their association with their friend and gaffer, Willie

Arrol. Right to the end, Arrol had been as ready to hold the end of a measuring tape for the most junior apprentice as he had been to discuss the erection of 500 tons of steelwork with his leading foreman. His employees never forgot the man who had always remembered them. Friendly co-operation had its reward. Arrol's employees practised what he preached; they took pride in their work, and the name of the firm became synonymous with all that was best in bridge engineering. They built the longest and the mightiest bridges spanning the Tay and the Forth, the heaviest over the Wear, and the most famous, the Tower Bridge over London's river. The knighthood conferred upon Arrol after the opening of the Forth Bridge on 4 March 1890 by Queen Victoria, was, apart from the recognition of Arrol's skill, an acknowledgement of the culmination of the long uphill struggle to put the engineering profession in this country back at the top. The black mark it had had from the ignominious fall of Bouch's Tay Bridge had been wiped out.

The present railway bridge over the Tay, officially called the Tay Viaduct, Dundee, carries a double line of railway and is 10,527 ft long. W. J. Gordon, in his well-known book *Our Home Railways*, described the Tay Bridge as having no architectural distinction, a monotonous erection redeemed from ugliness by its dimensions and the curve at the Dundee end. Excluding seven masonry arches, there are 79 girder spans of lengths varying from the thirteen 245-footers, the "high" spans of the through type, to 162 ft, 145 ft, 129 ft, 118 ft, 71 ft and 66 ft of the deck type. It is sited 60 ft upstream from the stumps of Bouch's piers, and the height of the girderwork over the navigation openings is 77 ft above high water level and 11 ft lower than the old single-line bridge. Bouch's bridge had been opened in May 1878, crossed by Queen Victoria in June 1879 and blown down in the following December.

Featureless, the Tay Railway Bridge may seem to some; in fact, the same adjective has been applied to the fine new Tay Road Bridge of modern times. But, in the history of bridge engineering, the railway crossing of the wide and stormy waters of the Firth of Tay was an important milestone.

William Arrol was the contractor for the world's longest (at that time) railway girder bridge. It was not his first great work. One of his earlier contracts and one on which Arrol left his mark, was the Caledonian Railway bridge over the Clyde outside Central Station in Glasgow. There, while building 2110 tons of wrought iron into the

three 4-track lattice girder through type spans, 142 ft, 185 ft and 164 ft
long, he made two far-reaching contributions to the practice of riveting ironwork. It was the first instance of mass-drilling six or more plates
in a single operation, instead of the old fashioned and time-consuming
habit of taking each plate separately to the drilling machines. Secondly,
that first of the Caley's bridges at the Broomielaw which was taken
away in 1966, was where Arrol first tried out his then newly-invented
scissor hydraulic riveting machines. With this mechanization, he stepped
up the number of rivets closed in a single working day to 1500; and
none was smaller than ¾ in. And what was even more important, the
powerful squeeze of 25 tons ensured that every rivet was sound.

The Clyde bridge had been started in May 1876, and it was finished
by 1 October 1878. The cost of the girderwork, fabricated and erected,
was only £16 10s. per ton. And if we include the substructure work
(there were 1350 tons of cast iron in the pier cylinders), the cost of the
whole bridge came to less than £2 per square foot of deck area. These
phenomenally low figures testified to the ability of this hardy Scottish
engineer who was showing the world the advantages to be gained by
mechanization.

The Tay Bridge offered Arrol even more scope for the use of improved practices. With seventy-three piers to build in the tidal waters,
Arrol devised floating platforms which were to all intents and purposes
the forerunners of the rigs used by the oil companies of today in their
search for oil and gas under the North Sea. These floating platforms,
complete with cranes, workshops, shelters for the men, and the gear
necessary for sinking the pier cylinders of the bridge 30 ft and more
into the bed of the Tay, could be moved on the water from pier to
pier; and then when located over the place where the couple of cylinders for a particular pier were to be put down, the platform lowered its
own four legs on to the river bed and lifted itself clear of the tides.
Arrol's movable platforms were more than 81 ft long and just under
66 ft wide, and their legs, located, one at each corner, were 6 ft in
diameter swelling out to "feet" measuring 12 ft across at the bottom.
These legs were 65 ft long, and by means of hydraulic gear the platforms could be raised well clear of the water while work on a pier was in
progress, and, lowered down with legs and feet drawn up, floated to
the next pier. A clever design permitted the platform to "un-dock" so
that it could be floated clear of the pier which it had just been used to

build. Arrol made four of these floating platforms, and with them he founded 73 pairs of cylinders and handled:

2300 tons of wrought iron cylinders,
680 tons of temporary caissons,
26,000 cubic yards of excavations,
6500 cubic yards of brickwork,
27,000 cubic yards of concrete, and
22,000 tons of cast iron blocks to weight the cylinders.

In the official report on the work, credit is given to Arrol for the design and construction of these movable platforms which "proved equal to all the work required from them, and withstood the boisterous weather and strong currents of the Tay without any mishaps".

With commendable Scottish care for the cost of a bridge, it was decided to re-use the girderwork of the old bridge which had remained standing after the disaster of December 1879, and incorporate it in the new spans. This meant transferring more than 100 girders from the old piers to the new structure. It had been proposed to skid them across on temporary trestle work, but the old girders were too slender for such treatment, one at a time. Arrol floated them on pairs of pontoons, the same way he used to float out all the new girders.

The new girders of the through type spans were put together and built into the complete 245-ft long spans, on a jetty built out from the south shore, the more sheltered shore, of the Tay. Then, only 12 ft above the water, they were floated on pontoons and taken by tugs to their appointed piers, where they were landed on timber blocks resting on the brickwork. Eventually, span by span, the new girderwork was raised by hydraulic jacks, and the superstructure of the piers, itself prefabricated in sections of malleable iron forming two octagonal pillars to be connected at the top by a semicircular arch, completed underneath the girderwork.

The Tay Bridge was a back-cloth. The stage was set for Arrol's greatest and most spectacular act at the crossing of the Forth, less than three years later. Without ceremony but probably not without the Queen's notice, the Tay Bridge was opened on 20 June 1887, the fiftieth anniversary of Her Majesty's accession. On 4 March 1890, H.R.H. The Prince of Wales was to drive the last rivet and formally declare open the Forth Bridge, mightiest of all railway bridges.

The Forth Bridge will never be equalled or surpassed for the simple reason that newer modes of transport which have supplanted the railway train do not require such tremendous girder structures. The building of the Forth Bridge of riveted steelwork, more than 50,000 tons of it fashioned and put together on site, symbolized the peak of the era of great railway bridges. The work was so stupendous that no book about girder bridges can afford to be without a separate chapter devoted to this most majestic of all bridges.

We pass on now to the heaviest railway girder bridge in the kingdom. Although the use of the greatest possible amount of steel may not be the goal of a good designer, the building of the Queen Alexandra Bridge over the river Wear at Sunderland was very much to the credit of Sir William Arrol. This bridge, built to carry a double line of the North Eastern Railway and a main road for the Corporation of Sunderland across the river at a point about 2½ miles above the entrance to Sunderland harbour, was opened by the Earl of Durham, K.G., on 10 June 1909, and by the gracious permission of Her Majesty the Queen it was named the Queen Alexandra Bridge. The primary reason for the building of this great bridge was the transportation across it by rail of 6 million tons of coal for export every year. That trade no longer exists, and the bridge which includes the longest and heaviest single span in Britain has long since ceased to have any railway trains crossing its deck.

Except for its weight, the Queen Alexandra Bridge is not unusual. It has three 200-ft land spans and a single one of 330 ft clear over the river where the clearance above high water at spring-tides is 85 ft. The main girders of all these spans are described as trusses of the Linville type; the chords of the land spans are straight, the top chord of the river span girders are hogged. The railway tracks were on an upper deck, the roadway separate, below. Each land span contained 1000 tons of mild steelwork; and the total weight of steelwork in the river span is 2600 tons, or nearly 7·9 tons of girderwork for every foot of length. If the dead weight of the permanent way, road-surfacing, etc., be added, the total weight comes to 3200 tons, which is equal to 9 tons per lineal foot. In this span, each main girder weighs 954 tons; and in the words of the paper "The Queen Alexandra Bridge over the River Wear, Sunderland" by F. C. Buscarlet and Adam Hunter (*Mins. Proc. Inst. C.E.* vol. 182, 1909–10, pt. IV), the weight of the river span was not exceeded by any existing bridge of the same length.

The contract for building and erecting this bridge was undertaken by Sir William Arrol & Company. It took four years to complete, and the total cost of the bridge which included lengthy approach works was about £325,000. Shipbuilding yards on both sides of the river extend close up to the bridge, and, in fact, new vessels are launched directly under it. So the contract for the building of the bridge contained a clause prohibiting any interference with the waterway while the river span was being erected.

Adam Hunter, later chief engineer of Sir William Arrol & Co., Ltd., and author of a well-known engineer's compendium of bridge-formulae and other data, devised and supervised the scheme for erecting the steelwork.

The contract suggested two alternative methods by which the river span might be erected. These were:

(1) By using temporary towers and suspension members attached to the bottom booms and anchored to the land spans. (Fortunately, the land spans were disposed so the river span was flanked by one on the south, and by two on the north.)

(2) By using the land-span girders cantilevered over the river, strutted out from the piers and anchored firmly to the shore, supporting a platform upon which the main girders might be erected.

Fortunately, the contractor was not bound to adopt either. He was left free to use his own ingenuity and put forward a better erection scheme provided it met with the approval of Charles A. Harrison, the Chief Engineer of the North Eastern Railway.

As so often happens, the contractor who lives and moves so much closer to the practical problems confronting the man on the job than the theorist chair-borne in his office, did have a better notion of how to get two-and-a-half thousand tons of bridgework across an open stretch of water. Arrol's scheme was to convert the main girders temporarily into cantilevers anchored back to the adjoining land spans, and to build them by overhang from each side of the river.

Harrison, who was a nephew of Thomas Elliot Harrison, Robert Stephenson's assistant, and a practical man himself, approved the scheme at once. The pity of the thing was the wasting of money on unnecessary steelwork. If only Arrol's method of erection had been thought of before the girderwork had been designed, many hundreds of tons of the steel that was built into the Queen Alexandra Bridge would not have been needed.

After the bridge had been completed, it was tested under a load of twelve steam locomotives making a total weight of 1190 tons or 3·34 tons per lineal foot on the double tracks. Under this very heavy test load, the central deflection of the river span was as little as $\frac{15}{16}$ in.

That the bridge had been well and soundly made there was no doubt whatever; but, whether the engineers had used their client's money to the best advantage is another matter. As an eminent engineer said during a learned discussion about the Queen Alexandra Bridge, the question of erection should have been the governing factor both in determining the most suitable type of girder to use and in the design of the bridge generally. The apparent neglect of this obvious step until after the design had been prepared, had resulted not only in the waste of unnecessary steelwork in the bridge proper but also in the temporary works needed to erect it. The only practicable method of erecting the bridge had been by transforming the girders into cantilevers, and the steelwork which had been required for the temporary towers and tie-backs, could have been more economically employed in a permanent and much lighter cantilever bridge.

Of course, it is easy to be wise after the event. However, the story of the Queen Alexandra Bridge does draw attention to the duty of every discerning bridge engineer, namely always to plan ahead and be wise before it is too late.

CHAPTER 12

Bridging the Forth

THE Forth Bridge, the cantilever bridge carrying the two railway tracks, was opened on 4 March 1890.

The Forth Road Bridge, the suspension bridge carrying two 24-ft wide carriageways, cycle track and footway was opened by Her Majesty Queen Elizabeth II on 4 September 1964.

Both are magnificent bridges, examples of the best engineering practice at the time of their construction. Both, by 1967 standards, are out of date. The railway bridge is riveted, and riveting, like the railway steam engine, has been superseded. The road bridge is old-fashioned, too; although it is of welded construction, its stiffening trusses and its deck, steel plate on the 3300-ft span and reinforced concrete on the two side ones, are built up of many parts and belong to the conventional suspension bridge design of by-gone riveting days.

In contrast, the latest railway and road bridges crossing the Wye and the Severn near Chepstow show the enormous advantages to be gained when engineers building welded steelwork break away completely from ideas which have for many years dominated designs whenever bridges were riveted. With a centre span only 60 ft shorter than the Forth Road Bridge, the Severn Bridge steelwork which carries the same standard of highway loading, weighs less than half that in the Scottish bridge.

Improvements in bridge design made since 1960 are really quite extraordinary. But this does not lessen our admiration for the achievements of the workers of a forgotten age who with no electricity apart from an unreliable lighting system of rather doubtful benefit, no internal combustion engine, and no handy portable compressed-air tools, erected more than 50,000 tons of steel plates and rolled sections in the three great cantilever towers and the two 1710-ft long spans of the Forth Bridge.

Sir John Fowler and Benjamin Baker (he was knighted afterwards) designed it. William Arrol assisted by Sir Thomas Tancred, baronet and engineer, put it up. Which was the greater achievement, it is hard to say; the preparation of hundreds of detail drawings and calculations in their Westminster office and the superintendence and continuous control over the entire operation of building the bridge, by the engineers; or the carrying out of the actual work on site. Both were stupendous undertakings with the reputation of the whole industry at stake. Perfection in the engineers' design made the contractor's work straightforward; thoroughness and attention to every process, from the initial marking-off of the plates and sections to the final riveting, coupled with an ability to solve the problems of handling heavy parts and machinery in awkward places, on the part of the contractor, meant the job would go through with a minimum of anxiety.

The fabrication of the steelwork needed a space of 60 acres on the south side. Few were the numbers of pieces of steel which could be handled without some sort of lifting appliance. Every limb of the three great cantilever structures had to be served by cranes crawling upward and outward as the particular member grew. There were steam cranes, hydraulic cranes, giant riveting cages, heavy hydraulic "scissor" riveting machines and all the paraphernalia common to the needs of men engaged in drilling, reamering, shaping, cutting and fitting steelwork together; and all had to creep ever outward and upward along those members. Power to operate the plant came not through wires or even air-hoses; neither dynamo nor pneumatic compressor was available in the contractor's kit; coal and water for the cranes had to be delivered to all parts of the girderwork; rivet-heating furnaces weighing half a ton apiece were run on oil-fuel, and yet another sign of the times, electric light was tried, with mixed results. The last was an arrangement of arc lights of between 1500 and 2000 candle-power, which proved to be quite hazardous because of their unreliability. Men working out on the erection would one minute be working in the dazzling glare of these lights and in the next they would be in a darkness made the more absolute by the sudden failure of a carbon. Such conditions cannot have added to the safety of men clambering about at night on the narrow slippery stagings and facing the cold and wet of a Scottish winter. Strangely, the effects of wind and rain are not mentioned in the records of the building of the railway bridge. It was to be left to the men on the catwalks of the road bridge, seventy years later, to experience the full effects of exposure to the icy gales that sweep across this open seaway; they were to lose one day out of every three working days spent spinning the cables for the most northerly of all the world's great bridges. In the cold bleak days and nights when the men of the Victorian period toiled to put the steelwork of the railway bridge together, they too suffered from the weather; but it was the effect of frost on the hydraulic machines and pipes that gave them the most trouble.

There is a link between the Royal Albert Bridge at Saltash and the Forth Bridge. John Fowler, joint designer of the Scottish bridge, had been appointed as consulting engineer to the Great Western Railway when Isambard Kingdom Brunel died in 1859.

Fowler, born in 1817 at Sheffield, gained his early training under an hydraulics engineer. He was thirteen when the Liverpool & Manchester Railway was opened; and a few years later he was caught up in the rush of the railway mania. Fowler became chief assistant in the office of J. U. Rastrick, one of the eminent engineers who gave evidence before the Commission enquiring into the use of iron in railway bridges in 1847. During the next thirty years, John Fowler was to be associated with almost every major railway project in the United Kingdom. In 1865 he became President of the Institution of Civil Engineers. In 1869 he accompanied the Prince and Princess of Wales on a journey up the River Nile and explained to his royal host and hostess the probable methods employed in ancient times for raising the large stones used in building the pyramids and temples. In 1885 Queen Victoria created Mr. Fowler Knight Commander of the Order of St. Michael and St. George "for important services and guidance to Her Majesty's Government in connection with Egypt". The Forth Bridge was to become the greatest work with which Sir John Fowler was associated.

If Sir John was the father of the project, Baker, his partner and twenty years his junior, is aptly described as the very active son in the business.

By the time Benjamin Baker came upon the scene, the great pioneers of the profession had, most of them, either passed away or retired. According to contemporary writers, engineering had been reduced to a science that replaced the more or less hit-and-miss experimental pursuit which had occupied the previous generation, and the foundation had been securely laid for the development of the profession which had already won world-wide distinction. Iron had given way to steel, and engineers were enabled to carry out successfully, undertakings which their immediate predecessors could not seriously contemplate for want of the proper materials.

Whereas Sir John Fowler had begun his professional training with level and theodolite in the north of England, Baker started the hard way with a hammer and chisel in Neath Abbey works, one of the oldest ironworks in South Wales, where, a hundred years before, Trevithick's earliest Cornish pumping engines had been made. In an atmosphere where the steam engine was being applied to railways, ships, mines and rolling-mills, Benjamin Baker learned to become an engineer; a further period elsewhere, levelling, surveying, and designing works in masonry and brickwork, brought him to London and so to Fowler's office where amongst other works he was engaged in building the Metropolitan Railway. Baker received his knighthood in recognition of his part in bridging the Firth of Forth. Five years later, Sir Benjamin Baker, K.C.B., K.C.M.G., D.Sc., LL.D., M.A.I., F.R.S., was elected President of the Institution of Civil Engineers.

William Arrol was apprenticed to a blacksmith in Paisley at the age of thirteen. He spent four years learning his trade; and, when he did become a journeyman, Scotland was paralysed by a financial crisis, and he went away south in search of work. Arrol was an optimist. He spent his time acquiring a varied stock of knowledge and saving money for the day when times would be better and he could set up on his own in business on his native heath. Whether working as a blacksmith, a fitter, or a boilermaker, Arrol did his work well. Always his work was characterized by that touch of originality which distinguished the man born to lead from the one born only to obey. Speaking at a gathering of friends from whom he had received a token of their esteem, when the Forth Bridge was nearing completion, Arrol said: "Whatever I went to I put my whole mind to. Sometimes I was sent to clean the flues instead of repairing the boilers, but I never shirked the duty." After rising from man-of-all-work to foreman of the bridge and boiler works of Laidlaw & Sons, of Glasgow and Edinburgh, Arrol thought the time had come for him to set up on his own. It was 1870. He launched

himself as a contractor and repairing engineer, with a capital of £85—
the savings of his life. He bought a steam engine for £18, a boiler for
£25, and the few tools he could afford. Within three years he had been
entrusted with contracts for the supply and erection of iron girder
bridges on the Glasgow, Hamilton and Bothwell Railway. The Caledonian Railway Bridge over the Clyde outside Glasgow Central, and
the reconstruction of the Tay Bridge followed, bringing Arrol into the
front rank among bridge builders of repute. Queen Victoria conferred
a knighthood on Sir William Arrol in 1890 after he had built the
Forth Bridge. Never was an honour more richly deserved.

Both the road and the railway crossings of the Firth of Forth were
preceded by thoughts about building long-span bridges across the
Severn estuary. In 1864, Fowler and Baker had put forward proposals
for a steel bridge, steel, note, not wrought iron, with a span of 1000 ft,
to carry the South Wales & Great Western Railway across the Severn.
A little later, with their design altered to a bridge of two 600-ft long
spans, an Act was obtained and a contract actually let for the construction of that Severn railway bridge; but the scheme never got off the
ground because of financial difficulties. Again, in 1871, these intrepid
designers put forward yet another plan. This time it was a bridge again,
there were to have been two spans, each 800 ft long. But, like its prede-
cessor, that particular Severn railway bridge never got beyond the
drawing-board stage; the Great Western Railway had, by then,
acquired the Bristol & South Wales Union Railway together with an
erratic steamboat ferry service across the estuary, and in 1872 they
obtained parliamentary powers authorizing the construction of a
tunnel under the river. The Severn Tunnel, 7664 yd long and the
longest ever to have been worked by steam locomotives on a railway
in Britain, was the child of Sir John Hawkshaw, engineer. It took 13½
years to build, and was opened in September 1886.

Fowler and Baker took their long-span bridge designs up north.
After the Tay Bridge disaster and the abandonment of Sir Thomas
Bouch's plans for the Forth Bridge, they were invited to prepare a
scheme for bridging that Scottish firth. Actually, Harrison, Barlow,
Fowler & Baker, as the firm was called, produced two designs. Both
had three lofty towers carrying balanced cantilever arms; but, in one
which had two great spans, each 1730 ft long with 500-ft suspended
girders, only the middle tower had four piers and would have been

"self-standing" without the need for auxiliary support during erection. In some respects this scheme followed the form of construction adopted for the Lansdowne Bridge across the Indus in India, which had given its erectors such a lot of trouble. That Indian railway bridge with its 850-ft span, had the distinction of being the world's longest during the eleven months immediately prior to March 1890 when the Forth Bridge was opened.

Fowler and Baker's second design, the one we see and admire so much today, had one distinct advantage over their alternative. All three towers were "free-standing"; each had four piers, and could be erected together with the cantilever arms, without the need for any temporary supports below.

Three-quarters of a century later, when the Forth came to be spanned by a road bridge, the work was carried out in accordance with plans which, once again, had in the first place been intended for a bridge over the Severn. Where Scotland gained in time in 1964, Wales gained in an improved design of bridge two years later. Though, here, one must hasten to point out that both ends of the great Severn Road Bridge which Her Majesty Queen Elizabeth II opened on 6 September 1966, are in England's Gloucestershire. It is the girders of the adjoining via-duct across the Beachley peninsular and the River Wye, that do not end until the road has reached Monmouthshire, and some say that is in Wales.

The Forth Bridge was the first bridge to use circular tubes for its principal strut members, since Brunel had built his railway bridge across the Wye at Chepstow. But both at the Wye and the Tamar bridges, Brunel had fashioned and finished the tubes, 9 ft diameter at Chepstow and oval, 16 ft 9 in. × 12 ft 3 in. at Saltash, on the ground and launched them afterwards. He prefabricated them. In the Scottish bridge, every part of the tubes was put into place by the platers and riveters building the giant members in the air. None of Arrol's bridge was prefabricated; compared with Brunel's, his task was much the more complex.

When Arrol first took on the work of bridging the Forth, they were building a bridge of two 1600-ft long spans as designed by Bouch before his ill-fated Tay Bridge brought his efforts into disrepute. In fact, of the whole sum of £3,227,206 spent on bridging the Forth for the railway, £250,000 had been expended in connection with Bouch's suspension bridge (including parliamentary expenses), and £378,000 spent in

PLATE 15. An M–U diesel train speeds across the "high girder" spans of the Tay Bridge.

PLATE 16. Underneath the deck-type spans of the Tay Bridge the stumps of the piers of Bouch's ill-fated bridge are framed between one of the original girders and a massive column supporting the present-day bridge.

PLATE 17. Mightiest bridge of all. More than six million rivets hold the parts of the Forth Bridge together.

PLATE 18. The heaviest span of all. Trains no longer use the upper deck of this 2600-ton span of the Queen Alexandra Bridge across the River Wear at Sunderland.

PLATE 19. Three-quarters of a century separate the Fife cantilever of the Forth Bridge and the cable of the great road suspension bridge of 1964.

PLATE 20. The open road of the twentieth century. One of the two 24-ft wide carriageways of the great 3300-ft span of the Forth Road Bridge.

PLATE 21. The only suspension bridge on British Rail. A G.W.R. "County" class 4-6-0 heads west across the Royal Albert Bridge. In 1968 a proposal was put forward to strengthen this historic bridge to enable trains of 100-ton trucks of china clay refuse to be worked out of Cornwall.

PLATE 22. All that remains of Bouch's bridge that was to have spanned the Firth of Forth. The stump of a pier carries a navigation light close by Inchgarvie.

meeting parliamentary charges and the interest on capital invested in the cantilever bridge project. The contract for the construction of the Forth Bridge, as we know it today, was let on 21 December 1882. It took seven long years to complete; and, at one time, 5000 men were engaged on the job. The working hours, the record (*Engineering*, 28 February 1890) tells us, were from 6 a.m. till 5.15 p.m., and from 5.45 p.m. until 5.45 a.m. for the night shift. No deduction was made for meal hours during the night, the full twelve hours being paid for. Fifty-seven men lost their lives in the building of the bridge.

The Quebec Bridge over the St. Lawrence river, has a single span of 1800 ft which is longer than either of the two great spans of the Forth Bridge. It, too, was built to carry a double line of railway, but already the changing demands of transport have resulted in one track being taken up and replaced by a roadway on the Canadian bridge. The length of the two great spans of the Scottish bridge exceeds the single span of Sydney's "coat-hanger" arch by 60 ft.

The successful completion of the Forth Bridge wiped out the disgrace that had been brought to the structural industry of this country by Bouch's miserable narrow-gutted high girders across the Tay. By the Forth Bridge and the new Tay Viaduct the East Coast railway route had clipped 37 miles off the journey to Aberdeen; Scotland acquired an additional tourist attraction, and a picture for her bank notes; statisticians learned that the repainting of the 145 acres of steel surface at the Forth Bridge is accomplished once in every three years; and the British bridge-builder was given the finest advertisement for riveted steelwork he is ever likely to receive.

The Forth Bridge will never be repeated. Time marches on. Riveting and railways fade into the background, victims of progress. That a majestic looking structure as remarkable as the Forth Bridge should be eclipsed by a suspension bridge containing, at the time of its opening, the longest bridgespan outside North America, seems logical enough. Victoriana has been supplanted by the modern Elizabethan age; surely that was to be expected. But when, in the course of only two years and a bit, Scotland's pride, namely the second Forth bridge, the Forth Road Bridge, is surpassed by a bridge of nearly similar length yet containing less than half the amount of steelwork, it is time to sit up and take notice. The rapidity of progress in British bridge design *is* something to shout about.

T.G.B.—D

The Forth Road Bridge is held up by two steel cables each containing 11,618 parallel wires 0.196 in. diameter. By means of more than 16½ miles of socketed wire rope hangers, these cables support a steel frame structure weighing 16,100 tons over two side spans, each a quarter of a mile long, and a middle span of 3300 ft. The two 512 ft high towers which hold the cables aloft are made of 5600 tons of welded steelwork. In contrast with Arrol's masterpiece, the whole of the twenty-one-and-a-half thousand tons of steelwork in the road bridge was prefabricated. It came from the workshops of five different companies. The towers came from the Dalmarnock Iron Works of Sir William Arrol & Co. in Glasgow who also made over a thousand tons of the suspended structure; the rest came from The Cleveland Bridge & Engineering Co. at Darlington, Dorman Long (Bridge & Engineering) Ltd., at Middlesbrough, Redpath Brown & Co. Ltd., and the Tees-side Bridge Co. All the shop-work was welded; the site-joints were "high-strength friction-grip" bolted, except for some welding of the deck plates; and there is not a single rivet in the whole bridge.

The numbers of men needed to put the Forth Road Bridge up never approached 10 per cent of the armies of workers employed to build the railway bridge. Twice, the labour force on site reached a peak of just over 400 men. But, remember, all the parts of the road bridge were prefabricated before they left the makers' workshops.

H. Shirley Smith, author and builder of many of the world's great bridges, was the contractors' agent on site when the Forth Road Bridge was being built. Throughout the work, safety measures for the workmen were considered of primary importance. The wearing of safety helmets was compulsory for everyone on the steelwork, and there were sets of safety harness for any men requiring them. In these precautions, the difference between the scaffolding moved about all over the girderwork in the older bridge, and the greater degree of security on the bridge made of prefabricated parts is very marked; but, alas, in spite of all the precautions on the road bridge, three men met their death during its construction. Ironically, two were killed in a mishap to a piece of safety equipment, the failure of a safety net assembly; and the third fatality happened through a one-in-a-million chance, when one of a pair of winches being used to lower a painters' gantry ran away causing a gear wheel to fly to bits. A piece of the flying metal hit the unfortunate victim, who was standing more than 30 ft away from the winch, on the head just below his safety helmet, killing him instantly.

The 1890 bridge has stood four-square to the gales for more than three-quarters of a century; never in that time have trains been stopped from crossing on account of the wind. And where the lateral deflection at the ends of the cantilever arms in a 100 mile an hour gale is measured in inches, the centre of the suspended structure of the road bridge is expected to move sideways more than 20 ft. This contrast in the flexibility of the two great bridges continues in the loadings each can carry. Loads up to 180 tons in weight can cross both bridges; on the railway, the carrying wagon would occupy a length of nearly 200 ft; on the road, it would cross on four-wheeled axles of a vehicle with a wheel-base of only 32 ft. The inflexible loading gauge on the railway would restrict the width of an out-of-gauge load; while on the road bridge, loads more than 24 ft in width could be taken across, subject to little more inconvenience than the wrath of other road-users temporarily prohibited from using the bridge.

There is a spaciousness about the road bridge which is not to be found in the Forth Bridge. The restrictiveness of a pair of running rails seems to have no place in the wide-open highway bridges of the second half of the twentieth century; but for all that, men will go on being drawn to the shores of the Forth to gaze in awe at the greatest railway bridge on earth, monument to the riveting age in bridge construction. Fifty thousand tons of steelwork erected and riveted up for only £6 17s. 9d. a ton.

CHAPTER 13

Reconstructing Chepstow Bridge "Land" Spans

EVERY bridge has an ultimate loading capacity. It can carry weights and forces up to that limit without failing; but the exact determination of what loading will cause that limit to be reached is not easy. Obviously, if the loading effects of trains are nearing the limit beyond which something catastrophic might happen, steps have to be taken to curtail the strains occurring in the bridge. Usually, the first step is to restrict speed. This minimizes the effects of impact caused by unevenness in the track, the lurching of rolling-stock, and, in the case of reciprocating engines, the hammer-blow effect of the out-of-balance forces in the locomotive. Other steps include the elimination of rail-joints on the bridge, propping the girderwork from below, the use of lighter rolling-stock, and so on.

The margin of safety between the heaviest loading authorized to cross the bridge, and the loading which would be just sufficient to bring about its downfall, is referred to as the factor of safety. It has often been called the factor of ignorance. Expressed numerically, the factor of safety is the ratio:

$$\frac{\text{the ultimate loading which would damage the bridge}}{\text{the heaviest loading authorized}}$$

If a steel bridge can stand strains caused by stresses of 27 tons/in^2 and no more, and the trains using it cause stresses of up to 9 tons/in^2, the factor of safety may be said to be 3. However, if the bridge is to survive an infinite number of similar loadings and the tensile stress is never to exceed $15\frac{1}{2}$ tons/in^2 (Chapter 1), the factor of safety comes down to 1·72.

The variations in the stresses at different places on a bridge are legion; the variations in the loading caused by the rolling-stock will not be known exactly; and the ultimate breaking stress of the components of the girderwork will not be known within plus or minus 5 per cent. Yet the factor of safety must not be allowed to approach unity; and the bridge engineer must give warning if the ratio is getting too close. Often instances occur of bridges continuing in service with factors of safety of as little as 1·5. Familiarity is apt to breed contempt. And when a bridge that has been carrying the same class of locomotive, day in and day out, for years seems perfectly sound although the actual factor of safety may be even less than 1·5, it is often difficult for an engineer to convince the managers of the railway that they really must face up to either using a different class of motive power or incurring heavy expenditure on strengthening or reconstructing the bridge.

Such a state of affairs occurred at Chepstow in 1944. It was during the war years which had followed a long period of financial restraint. That, of course, was no excuse for allowing the factor of safety to approach unity. But in the main girders of the "land" spans, it did do just that.

These 300-ft long wrought iron girders had been carrying trains ever since 14 July 1852. It was the right-hand side main girder of the Down line which gave way close to where it took support from the first of the intermediate piers. It broke on 4 April 1944, a week after the Royal train hauled by two "Castle" class engines had crossed it. Whether the damage initiated from the passage of that particular train we shall never know for certain; but the running of "Castle" engines coupled together had been prohibited, and certainly the two engines did constitute a loading in excess of the normal run of the traffic.

The detection of the failing girder in the nick of time is told by T. B. C. Davies, the District Engineer at Gloucester, in a dramatic report to A. S. Quartermaine, the Chief Engineer, whose wartime headquarters were at Aldermaston:

"At approximately 09.00 a.m. the Sub-Ganger of the length noticed the ballast boards (the boards which kept the ballast away from the girderwork) on the 6-foot side (the area between the tracks of a double-line railway in Britain is generally referred to as the 'six foot', although the actual measurement seldom bears much resemblance to fact) of the Down line, some ninety feet from the Chepstow end main pier of this bridge had lifted. He raised the boards and found the web of the girder showing signs of buckling. While doing this, he noticed trains approaching on both roads. He climbed on to the top of the centre girders and, when the trains passed, noticed the girder carrying the Down line sag considerably.

"He went to the station (Chepstow) and, fortunately, found his Sub-Inspector and my Assistant (Frank Gibbons) who had just arrived on the Down train which left Gloucester at 09.00 a.m. and reached Chepstow at 10.13 a.m. My Assistant had noticed a lurch on crossing the bridge and hurried back to the site. The passage of the last train had apparently accentuated the damage.

"My Assistant immediately sent out the Sub-Ganger with instructions to stop any further trains on the Down road, and himself hastened to the station to see that no further trains were allowed on that road. He was just in time to have the signals set at danger against the next train which had already entered the block section. . . ."

The superstructures carrying the two tracks were separate on the Chepstow Bridge, and single-line working was allowed at severely restricted speed on the Up line. Ronnie Sargent was the Bridge Assistant in the Chief Engineer's office at the time, and it was largely to his credit that temporary repairs to the buckled girder were carried out with such expedition that double-line working was resumed on 24 April.

As constructed by Brunel, the plate girders of the "land" spans of the Chepstow Bridge were notorious for the slenderness of the webs. The girders were about $7\frac{1}{2}$ ft in height and they had curiously shaped top flanges formed of a single curved plate on the top with two sloping plates either side fashioned so as to form a triangle when viewed in cross-section. The sloping plates were riveted to the outer extremities of the curved plate, and to the web plate. Inside these hollow flanges, every third piece of web plate was continued on and up to meet an angle by which it was riveted to the middle of the curved plate. The distance between the top and bottom flanges was about 7 ft 6 in., and since 48 in. was about the greatest width of wrought iron plate obtainable in the days when these girders were being made, there were a great many vertical joints in the webs. Brunel had attached the cross girders, which carried a decking of longitudinal timbers and the ballasted railway tracks, to the lower 15 in. or so of these webs; but except for the stiffening effects of those connections, he left the webs unstiffened over lengths of more than 30 ft. This fact had not escaped notice, and at the turn of the century, following the appearance in the technical press of letters from eminent engineers who had doubted the security of these slender web plates, a number of additional stiffeners had been riveted onto the webs of the plate girders of both the "land" and the river spans.

Evidently, the stiffening had not been enough, and after Sargent had bolstered up the buckled girder with a pair of 100-ft long plate girders which he was just able to get in between the original girder and the trains (thanks, no doubt, to the generous clearance left by the old broad-gauge), a number of fresh stiffeners were added throughout the whole bridge.

Little else could be done during the war; but, as soon as hostilities ceased and things commenced to return to normal, orders went out that the six 100-ft "land" spans were to be renewed. Work on the Down line started early in June 1948, and those three spans were completed in nine weeks; the renewal of the Up line spans followed.

There was 600 tons of mild steel in the new spans, compared with 204 tons of wrought iron in the main girders of Brunel's six "land" spans. The whole of the new girderwork was fabricated and erected by the Fairfield Shipbuilding & Engineering Co. Ltd., Chepstow, successors to the firm of Edward Finch & Company who had come from Liverpool and set up works by the Wye at Chepstow when they made the iron work of the original bridge nearly a century earlier.

Unlike the wrought iron main girders of the old spans which were continuous over the two intermediate piers, the new steel girders were separate in each span. No doubt the idea stemmed from a belief that the fabrication of twelve girders, all more or less identical, would cheapen the cost; but the resulting increase in weight of steel required ran away with any saving there might have been. Moreover, the arrangement of two bearings on a tall 6-ft diameter cylinder, which proved to be remarkably flexible when relieved of any superstructure, was not nearly so good as the single bearing from Brunel's continuous girders which had brought the reaction fairly and squarely over the middle of the pier.

In each of the intermediate piers there were only three cylinders. So there was not enough room to spare for the new girders to be landed on the pier-tops before the old girders had been taken away; and towers of standard military unit-steel trestling were built up to give temporary support to the new girders which were delivered on rail-bogeys direct from the works nearby. There was nothing particularly outstanding about the method of erection. Each pair of new main girders was used to carry a runway of travelling beams from which the old girders were supported while they were cut into manageable lengths, about 15 ft long, and lowered down. Afterwards the new girders were slewed to their final centres, lowered on the pier-tops, and the new flooring riveted in position to complete the spans. One slight complication occurred with the girders of the spans adjacent to the river pier. There each girder had to be slid along into the pockets in the cast ironwork where they took their bearings.

Additional bracings were fitted between the cylinders of the two intermediate piers. This was done partly to restore some of the lateral stability lost when the girders ceased to be continuous across the three "land" spans.

The 1948 "land" spans of the Chepstow Bridge were among the last examples of riveted girderwork to appear on the Western Region of British Railways. Apart from the main girders themselves which were of course delivered as completely finished units, there was an enormous amount of site work involved in building the steel decks. It was a time of change. Already the technique of bridge-building in steel was undergoing fundamental changes brought about by the advances in steelwork fabrication evolved during the war. Arc-welding was superseding the hot-driven rivet; the race of men skilled in the riveting trade was dying out; the number of young men coming forward to learn how to close a rivet, on Clydeside alone, could be counted on the fingers of one hand. The year 1948 was also the year when nine main line bridges were swept away by floods on the Scottish Region between Berwick-on-Tweed and Edinburgh. Never before in the history of the East Coast Route had there been so complete a disruption of the services; with main line traffic diverted via Carlisle, and local trains running to severely restricted schedules over temporary bridges on the Berwick line, the opportunity was seized to go modern with the new and permanent girderwork. When the line was fully restored by 1951, the trains ran over welded steelwork, designed by the railway engineers in London and made by P. & W. Maclellan & Co. in Glasgow. The new-fashioned girderwork weighed between 13 and 21 per cent less than if it had been riveted, and in the case of a 69-ft long span the saving in cost was put at no less than 27 per cent.

It was a sign of the times. Steelwork fabricators and British Railways were crossing another bridge.

CHAPTER 14

The Half-through Type Bridge

THE half-through type of girder bridge, the one adopted so extensively in the early days because of the relatively small C.D. (construction depth) required with its form of construction, used to be the most ill-conceived and most maltreated of all the underline structures on the railways of Britain. The main girders were not directly below the trains; they were away to the side of the track. So the reaction from the floor, transverse timbers or corrugated troughing, cross-girders or what have you, transmitted a loading which was eccentric on the main girders; and because for many years the effects of this eccentricity remained almost totally ignored by designers, the half-through type bridge came to be regarded as one of the most troublesome forms of structure under the line.

At the 1847 Enquiry many of the experts said the eccentric loading caused by bearing the cross-beams on one side of the bottom flange of a girder did not really matter. Eminent engineers admitted there would be a twisting set up in the girders; but they persisted that the effects were of no consequence. This disregard for important stresses and strains was to cost the railways dearly. As a result, bridge designs were faulty; vital connections were not made strong enough; and because the joints between the floor and the main girders, not easy to look after at the best of times, were constantly being overstrained, maintenance charges rose steeply and often lead to an early replacement of the whole bridge.

To understand properly what was involved, it is as well to review two simple fundamentals in the science of structural engineering. A joint or connection intended by the designer to be rigid must be made strong enough to withstand *all* stresses without *any* part of the metal being overstrained; there must be no "give" in such a joint. If, on the other hand, this requirement of absolute rigidity cannot be met, as happens when the space is insufficient and the components cannot be made large enough, the parts meeting at the connection must have complete freedom of movement; or in other words, there must be nothing to prevent the joint behaving like a hinge; and wherever such movement takes place, the designer must make due allowance for the effects of wear.

Provision used not to be made for the wearing away of the surfaces of piers and abutments. Flat bearing plates riveted to the undersides of the girders rested directly upon the softer stone, concrete or brickwork; and, since movement takes place at the end of any beam deflecting under the passage of a load, it was only a very short time until the bearing plate had worn its way into the stone. It would not have mattered so much if the wear in the stone had been even all over, but it seldom was. It was a defect common to all kinds of girder bridges though the eccentric loading of the main girders rendered the half-through type of construction particularly susceptible to the trouble. The unevenness of the surface of the stone or brickwork underneath the bearing plate would eventually put a twist in the girders causing them to heel over to one side and overstrain connections to cross girders, bracings, and so forth. Knuckle bearings and stepped bearings in which the wear is confined to metal-on-metal surfaces, have cured the trouble; where they are fitted, the bedplate is dowelled to the top of the pier or abutment and there is no movement between the steel and the stone.

To return to the case of the half-through type of bridge with the cross-bearers either resting on the bottom flanges of the main girders or jointed into the webs. In its simplest form like the Portland Road Bridge at Norwood Junction involved in the L.B. & S.C.R. crash in 1891, the cross-bearers were of timber and they rested directly upon the bottom flanges of the cast iron main girders. These flanges projected more than 13 in. under the cross-bearers which were themselves 8 in. wide. No doubt, initially, the timbers would have been adzed and fitted to give an even bearing close against the webs of the main girders; but with movement taking place under the passage of every wheel of a train, it would not take long before the timbers settled down to bear on the very edges of the girder flanges. The cross-bearers were spaced

3 ft apart, and as the wear would hardly be likely to be the same under each timber, some would very soon be carrying more than their fair share of the loading. Inevitably, the strain on the main girders would be increased because the loading ceased to be properly distributed through the cross-bearers. That is probably what happened on that fateful morning in May.

This faulty design of the connections between the floor and the main girders was to persist right up until after the Second World War; that bible of every design office, the specification, for the design of girder bridges issued by the British Standards Institution, continued to call for cross girders to be considered as freely-supported beams spanning between the centre-lines of the main girders. The instruction was admirable as far as it went; no relief was to be claimed if the cross girder took a bearing near the edge of a flange. But the fact was overlooked that if the cross girder were to be designed as *freely* supported at its ends, it had to be quite free to move at each end. In technical parlance, the cross girder was to be free from any form of restraint at the ends; it was not to have to carry any bending stresses where it rested on the main girders.

Even before designers progressed away from the wooden cross-beam, they were bolting the beams to the cast iron girders to hold the parts together; and just as soon as they had made these bolted connections, they had introduced restraint. In the timbers this was not of much concern because the bolt holes soon eased a bit and no harm was done. But as soon as iron cross-girders were bolted or riveted to the main girders, real trouble started.

As a rule, the cross-girders in a half-through type bridge are very shallow because of the need to keep the C.D. as low as possible. Consequently, the cross-girder has a relatively large deflection under trains, and the ends, if there is the least tendency for restraint, will have to transmit the stresses caused by the bending of the connections. On the one hand the cross-girder is trying to deflect under the load, and on the other the main girder is trying to remain truly upright as it presses down on its own bearings.

Many engineers have appreciated this high stressing of the ends of cross-girders, and they have devised various "weak" connections which provide some "give" in the joints without actually showing failure. But the completely free bearing for the end of a cross-girder

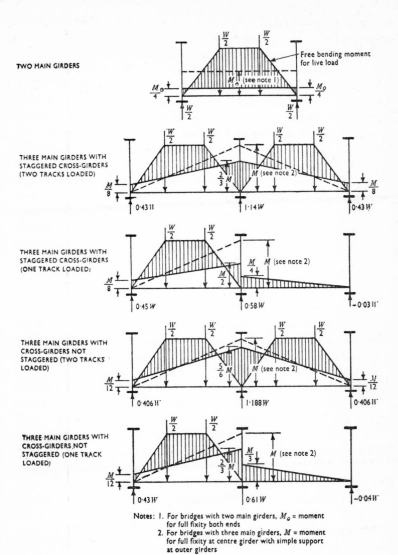

Notes: 1. For bridges with two main girders, M_o = moment for full fixity both ends
2. For bridges with three main girders, M = moment for full fixity at centre girder with simple support at outer girders

FIG. 12. Bending-moment diagrams for cross-girders in half-through type spans. The hatching indicates the magnitude of the bending-moments to be carried by the cross-girders.

fastened to a main girder eluded them. One of the nearest approaches to the ideal came with the introduction of trough decking. This plate flooring made strong through being corrugated became very popular because it could be used without cross-girders and would span across from one main girder to the other. Being comparatively shallow, it was most suitable when C.D. was very tight. The first applications of transverse troughing saw the bottoms of the troughs riveted or bolted to the flanges of the main girders while the "hills" of the troughs were cleated to the web of the main girder. This, of course, at once introduced a condition of complete restraint at the ends of the troughing which was asked to carry bending stresses it was quite incapable of sustaining. The result, cracks and splits in the trough plates and a black mark for the protagonists of transverse troughing. This was really very unfair to troughing. It should not have been blamed for a weakness caused by stresses for which it was not designed. So some concession was made. Bridges were put up with the troughing resting on but not fastened to the bottom flanges of the main girders, while connection was still maintained with the cleats riveted to the webs of the girders. This was an improvement so far as the troughing was concerned; but the wear under the "valleys" of the troughs was excessive, access for maintenance was difficult, and the troughing, distorted through the stretching of the overloaded rivets through the "hills" and the angle cleats, soon developed cracks.

Across bridges on railways in Britain, the tracks are nearly always ballasted if C.D. permits; and in an effort to improve maintenance conditions at the ends of transverse troughing, some engineers favoured a concrete haunching to keep the ballast away from the connections. This haunching hid the web of the girder and the top surface of the troughing from view altogether; so with the evils of the faulty connections hidden behind the concrete, it was a case of "out of sight, out of mind". This led to what became known at Paddington as a "Weston Rhyn".

A bridge about 30 ft long and spanning Telford's original London to Holyhead road near Weston Rhyn on the main line between Shrewsbury and Chester had three main girders and carried the two ballasted cross-sleeper tracks on transverse troughing. The condition where the troughing was attached to the middle one of the three main girders was about as bad as it could possibly be. When an Up train crossed the bridge, the middle girder would incline over towards that track; when a Down train passed, it went the other way; and when two trains crossed on the bridge, the connections of the troughing took a real pasting. Concrete haunching had been put in and matters did not look too bad to anyone walking along the track; the bridge had the merit of looking tidy. But, unfortunately, at this particular bridge the web stiffeners were stopped off just above the tops of the "hills" of the troughing; so, throughout the depth of the troughing, the web of that middle girder had nothing to stiffen it; the web was free to bend as it liked.

One day in October 1953, the ganger reported difficulty in keeping a good top on his road and complaints were received that stones from the ballast were falling through on to the road below. Reggie Barnwell, the District Engineer at Shrewsbury at that time, hurried out to see what was wrong. He found the web of that middle girder split over a continuous length of 19 ft just above the bottom flange angles. Again, it was a case of signals thrown to danger in the face of on-coming trains.

All traffic had to be suspended until trestling could be erected underneath—fortunately, there was room in the road—and the bridge propped up and made fit to carry trains at a severely restricted speed; and immediate steps were taken to order a new superstructure of welded girderwork.

Subsequently, assessment of the position showed there were more than 200 similar bridges which had been "protected" with concrete haunching, on the Western Region alone, and many more elsewhere on British Railways. Each could have been in the process of becoming a potential "Weston Rhyn".

CHAPTER 15

Welding instead of Riveting

An acute shortage of skilled riveters after the Second World War was, so far as bridge engineering is concerned, a blessing in disguise. It accelerated the advent of girder-fabrication by the process of joining steel plates together by the heat of the electric-arc. Welding was to become the greatest boon to the bridge builder since the riveted wrought iron girder had ousted the cast iron beam.

Some welding had been tried before 1939. On the former North Eastern Railway, welding had been used to repair old riveted bridges. And on London's Underground, the very first all-welded plate girder underline bridge—Hammersmith & City Railway Joint Committee Bridge numbered HC 3—had been brought into use just outside Ladbroke Grove Station.

Welding as a method of fastening steel plates and rolled sections together differed from riveting in two fundamentals. A rivet could be checked and tested by tapping with a hammer to see if it was sound; but in the early days of welding there was no way of being sure a weld did not contain some hidden flaw except by breaking it open. It was the case of the old cast iron beam with its hidden blow-holes, all over again. Secondly, whereas a rivet did "give" and even work loose without letting the girderwork fall apart, a weld was comparatively inflexible. A weld was either sound or it was unsound; quite firm or broken. There was no halfway about the welded joint; if the weld failed, the girder would fall down. Quite understandably, bridge engineers were reluctant to use a process about which they could not be sure.

The collapse of a road bridge of welded girderwork in Belgium did not help matters although the cause was attributed to the use of a steel unsuitable for welding. Brittle fracture came into prominence through the spectacular failure of some welded ships. At least one hull split in two from top to bottom while a ship lay tied up in dock. While welding was to blame for these failures, it was admitted that the designers had not appreciated the fundamental differences between the behaviour of plates welded together and those joined by rivets. The designers had not been able to break away from certain habits associated with riveted fabrication, the process for which they had been trained.

Actually, brittle fracture was not a new phenomenon. Riveted structures, ships included, can suffer the effects of brittle fracture if the internal stresses locked in in the girderwork during fabrication or in the steel during its manufacture, become too great. In riveted work, a split originating through brittle fracture is usually arrested at the nearest rivet hole; and the result, serious as it undoubtedly is, is unlikely to be catastrophic. In welded structures, there are no such crack-arresting holes; no riveted joints to act like safety-valves to ease off excessive stress. So, special care has to be taken in the design of welded steelwork to avoid any feature which might give rise to a high concentration of stress. By paying attention to these fundamental requirements in the design, and by specifying the use of a steel of a notch ductile quality immune from brittle fracture within the range of temperature likely to be met with at the site, it is possible to build a welded girder bridge which is every bit as safe and satisfactory as a riveted one, and a good deal cheaper.

London Passenger Transport Board used an all-welded super-structure for the three-girder 40-ft long double-track half through type plate girder bridge across Ladbroke Grove in 1938. Welded underline bridges had been built in Germany and Switzerland before that date, but so far as Britain was concerned, welding had been confined to the reconditioning and strengthening of existing bridges.

Although welding has its uses in the repair of riveted steelwork (and of riveted wrought iron, too, if care is taken to avoid separating the fibres of the metal), it is only in girderwork which has been designed specifically for fabrication by welding that the economic advantages of the process show up.

In 1938, the L.P.T.B. claimed to have saved more than 10 per cent in the dead weight of steel in their bridge at Ladbroke Grove; the total cost had come to £3849 compared with an estimate of £4186 for a riveted superstructure of the same strength; and they expected the the annual cost of maintenance of the welded girderwork to be £140 instead of £157 10s. On the other hand, the traffic over the Ladbroke Grove bridge was confined to electric multiple-unit passenger trains; the speed was low and there was none of the punishment suffered by bridges crossed by steam locomotives where hammer-blow and other troublesome forces added greatly to the impact effect.

The next big step forward in the use of welded girder bridges on British Railways came in 1948, after the breaches on the East Coast main line north of Berwick-on-Tweed (Chapter 13). There, there was no doubt about the economies; of the six tenders received for the supply of girderwork for eight bridges, the rates for riveted steelwork were, in every case, higher than for welded girders.

At about the same time, the Western Region engineers had been working on designs for a new kind of half-through type span in which the whole of the shop fabricaton was by welding while the girderwork was to be fastened together with high strength bolts when the bridge was being erected on site. This kind of bridge could not be completely prefabricated at the maker's works because, once put together in its entirety, it was too large to transport by rail. So it was imperative that some new fastener be found which would be suitable for making the permanent connections between the shop-welded and prefabricated parts, when a bridge was being erected on site.

Riveting had sufficed for these joints in the past, but the riveting process had always been far too slow. Had it not been for the enlarged pay-packets earned by bridge gangs working over week-ends, the riveted bridge might have disappeared years ago. Without the monetary benefits of Sunday work, many of the men employed by the railways would have taken work elsewhere. But, be that as it may, after Hitler's war there were no young men eager to learn riveting as a trade, and on some regions of British Railways it was almost impossible to find men capable of closing a rivet properly.

So, as a fastener, the rivet was taboo. One alternative might have been site welding, but it had several serious drawbacks. Good quality manual welding depends on ideal conditions. The operator must be fresh and fit, and he must be a conscientious and accomplished tradesman; he must not be hurried, and if the weather is cold or wet, both the steel and the human being must be warmed and kept dry. Such conditions are difficult to fulfil on an exposed site where men are struggling to get the parts of a bridge to go together within a brief occupation period between trains. And, equally difficult to contend with is the distortion of steelwork caused by welding; correction in the shops is very much easier than it is on a bridge site.

So, as a fastener for use in the field, welding was unacceptable.

Two other fasteners considered were the common mild steel black bolt and its refined cousin, the fitted bolt. The former could not be tightened sufficiently and it could not be depended upon to stay tight in a bridge subjected to vibrations under dynamic loading like a railway; it simply was not strong enough. The latter, the bolts with the shanks machined, which had to be a close fit in the holes, were far too expensive. The fitted bolt was a refined fastener depending upon an accuracy of fit seldom attainable in structural girderwork.

So, as a general-purpose fastener, neither the black bolt nor its machined counterpart were suitable for making the permanent joints in railway bridges.

Fortunately, at this time there appeared in the technical press reports of a revival in the U.S.A. of the technique of connecting steel parts together with bolts made of a much stronger kind of steel (it had a breaking strength of between 45 and 55 tons/in². The system, which had been invented before the First World War and had been abandoned because of the difficulty of obtaining bolts of sufficient strength, depended upon the vice-like grip—the friction-grip—of these high-strength bolts to develop the strength of the joint. In America, the technique had been applied with success to the joints in the steel structures of ore-handling plant; reports on how these bolts had remained perfectly tight under very exacting conditions, were most encouraging.

So, to cut a long story short, the high-strength friction-grip bolt came to be adopted, first of all on the Western Region and very soon afterwards throughout the whole of British Railways and the L.P.T.B., as the ideal fastener for the field connections between the prefabricated parts of steel bridges. Tightened either by hand with a geared spanner or by a machine-driven wrench, the high-strength friction-grip bolt supplied strictly in accordance with the specification, is very nearly foolproof. The diameter of the shank (it is not machined) is $\frac{1}{16}$ smaller than the hole, so a close-tolerance fit is not required; and since the method of tightening is extremely simple, it is not necessary to employ skilled labour to bolt the parts of bridges together.

One other advantage of the h-s f-g bolt is that it can be properly used in direct tension, that is to say it can be used under a loading which is tending to pull the nut away from the head. This is a boon to the designer seeking a fastener which can be used in a connection which has to resist bending forces like the joint between a cross-girder and a main girder. This use of the h-s f-g bolt is in contrast with the more usual shear-resisting function of the properly used rivet and the fitted bolt where the sliding apart of the steel plates is prevented by the resistance to shear of the shank and the hardness of the rivet, bolt and the metal surrounding the hole which bear against one another.

Eventually, the high-strength bolt was to become the field-joint fastener used throughout on the modern suspension bridges across the Tamar and the Forth, as well as in almost every power-station structure put up in the United Kingdom since the war. The engineers at Paddington took pride in the knowledge that their efforts in developing this useful fastener were to make a major contribution to modern practice in structural engineering; their specification for high-strength bolting was adopted as the basis on which the later standards for this system of fastening have been built up; and, in this, acknowledgement must be made to Mike Easton, one time shipwright, mathematician and naval architect, at Paddington for his painstaking care in formulating this important document.

That is not the end of the story. Indeed, it is not the beginning either. Several years after the adoption of the high-strength bolt as the standard fastener in steel bridges, the engineers in the Steelwork Office at Paddington found that by using the principle of friction-grip, they had merely revived a theory which the first chief engineer of the Great Western Railway had put forward more than a century before. At the 1847 Enquiry, Brunel had given evidence (Chapter 5) which included the following:

"I believe that in riveting plates together, where they will be exposed to tension, the rivets should not be considered as pins or bolts to be exposed to a cross strain, and holding the plates through which they pass merely as a bolt through the eye of a link, but they should be treated, and disposed accordingly, as clamps which compress the plates powerfully together, and produce an adhesion laying hold of the surface of the enclosed plate as if in a vice. . . ."

The only difference between Brunel's idea of 1847 and modern practice is that the fastener of today can be tightened so as to give a positive and exact grip based on predetermined requirements, which is very much stronger than the very varying clamping effect resulting from the cooling and contracting rivet of olden days.

To return to the subject of welded fabrication. It was not just a case of joining plates and sections together by melting the steel edges and fusing the parts instead of boring holes and pinning them together with rivets. The whole technique of fabrication by welding was different; and to get the best out of it, the designer had to try and forget how he used to plan for the joining of the parts of a riveted structure. He had to re-adapt himself to the new ways; and most important of all, he had to be very much more exact in determining the stresses his bridge was going to be subjected to. No longer could he ignore secondary and deformation stresses. If the joints between cross-girders and the main girders in a half-through type bridge were to be rigidly held with high strength bolts, the welded steelwork in the vicinity had to be strong enough to carry the strains set up through the end-restraint of the cross-girders. In the past, disregard of such forces had often led to loose rivets and corrosion-fatigue where the surface of the steel was over-stressed; but nothing more serious happened because the loosening rivet had allowed the overstrained joint to breathe. In welding, things were very different. The designer had now to be quite sure no part of his welded structure would be overstressed under any loading whether it was caused by the weight of trains, the thermal expansion and contraction of the girder-work, the locked-in forces in the steel or in the welded work itself, and so on. Henceforth, he could not afford to leave anything to chance; he would have to know about the behaviour of *all* parts of his bridges.

By 1946, advances made in methods of examining welds by radio-graphy and ultrasonics—an application of the echo depth-sounding technique used aboard ship—gave reliable non-destructive means of checking the internal structure of the welds. With these and with the introduction of periodical testing of welders by the physical bending and other ways of testing specimens prepared by them, the steelwork inspectors were able to keep a close watch on the quality of the welds and the standard of workmanship in the actual fabrication. Suspicions about welded girderwork were dispelled; and, in future, provided designs and specifications obeyed the new rules, there was no reason why a bridge made of welded steelwork should not be as reliable as one put together with rivets.

Within a few years, further improvements removed the chance of a welder producing work of a poor quality through the effects of human tiredness. Manual welding gave way to complete automation, the welder having little to do apart from setting up the machine and watching to see that it carried out his orders correctly.

With this new medium the bridge designer could now tailor his structures in such a way that they could be almost entirely prefabricated in the works. Assembly on site, reduced to the bolting up of a few joints, became so very much easier, quicker and cheaper. The days of frenzied drifting, bolting, reamering, unbolting and riveting to get a bridge together before the next train was due, were over. No longer would the quality of the workmanship, and therefore to some extent the efficiency of the structure, be at the mercy of the weather; not again would there be the need for riveting squads poised on flimsy scaffolds, hands numbed by the touch of freezing-cold steel. It was good-bye to awkward staging, the noisome rivet-gun, the chipping-hammer and the cumbersome portable drill with its bar and clamp.

The whole of the work to be done by skilled tradesmen could henceforth be completed within the warmth and shelter of the workshop. There, with light and power in plenty, and cranes, machines and every form of automation readily available, eyes, ears and muscles could be concentrated on the work in hand. The work was much more easily supervised. If anything was amiss, facilities were at hand to correct matters. It was only a short step further to improving the protection of the steelwork by completing the painting while it was still under cover in the shops.

In former days it had been customary to give the girderwork a single coat of red lead paint applied over the mill scale with which the surfaces were encrusted, and then to let the bridge "weather" for about a year before scraping it clean and giving it the full paint treatment. It was a thoroughly bad practice. Some of the mill scale would have come off, some would not; the "weathering" varied from surface to surface, and where the scale came off early, the steel would get thoroughly pitted with rust before it was painted. By the new painting-in-the-shop system, all the scale was removed before the paint was applied; the paint went on when the surface was clean and dry—which it seldom was out on the line where engine exhaust was nearly always at hand to give a deposit of damp and dirt even if it were not actually raining—and when every surface of the steel could be turned over and got at by the painter. After erection, it was a simple matter to touch up any places where the paint had been damaged during transit; such places were seldom the ungetatable parts which used to suffer so badly in the slap dash days of "weathering" the steelwork.

Painting in the shop naturally cost more in the first place because the girders occupied valuable floor-space for longer periods; but, with the intervals between painting increased from one year to eleven years to begin with, and from three years to eight or nine thereafter, the saving was very considerable. Besides, under the new system, steel bridges could be expected to last twice as long as they used to.

Welding cheapened the bridge in every respect. The drawings cost less to produce. The amount of detailing required by the man on the shop-floor was less. There were no rivet-pitches to have to work out to suit the spacing of stiffeners, the curtailment of flange plates, and so forth. The quantities of steel to be listed and ordered were down by 10 or 15 per cent; it was nearly all plates or universal flats with, perhaps, a small demand for rolled steel beams or joists. The contrast with the riveted bridge where the material lists would include many different sizes of equal angles, unequal angles, tees, channels and other rolled sections, was very marked.

In the template loft, the reduction in the number of holes in the parts of a bridge cut the work by nearly 90 per cent. In the shops, the centre-pop marking, the hole-punching, the drilling and reamering of the thousands of holes that had been the prelude to putting the parts of a plate girder together, all went by the board. The riveting gangs with their boys and the heating furnaces, the holders-up, the pom-pom hammers, the rivet squeezers and all the ancillary equipment of stitching bolts, spanners, washers, clamps and what not, began to disappear.

The workmen did not mind; there were no riveters to be put out of work. Newcomers to the industry had long since shown a preference for the welders' craft. But with management, the story was not quite the same. Controllers of long-established firms took longer to convince that batteries of drilling machines, the power and plant for closing rivets, and even their stocks of rivets, snaps and crows-foot chisels, were ceasing to be valuable assets.

Structural engineering had arrived at another bridge. In spite of a reluctance shown by some starters, it was a bridge few could afford not to cross. British Railways, thoroughly satisfied as to the reliability of the new form of construction, took industry by the hand and lead her across. It was the most important step forward since the days when Stephenson and Brunel had introduced the riveted wrought iron girder, more than 120 years ago. Forms of motive power and the names of the lines might change, but the go-ahead spirit of the pioneers lived on. Once again the railway engineers of this country were to give the lead to those concerned with keeping Britain's heavy industry out in front.

The Western Region engineers were especially fortunate. The descendants of the firm responsible for making Brunel's "tubular" bridge at Chepstow, namely the Fairfield Shipbuilding & Engineering Co., then a Branch of the Clydeside firm, had long been making riveted bridges for the Great Western Railway; and, about this time, the local directorship of Fairfields in Chepstow passed into the hands of Arthur Nicholas, a man who had spent all his working life making bridges with Fairfields.

Arthur knew a lot about making a riveted girder. The son of a Chepstow butcher, he had gone into the works as soon as he left school. Starting at the bottom, Arthur worked his way up the ladder; and on the way, the time and money consuming operations of matching holes, bolting up plates and sections, and riveting them, had not escaped his notice. In welding, Arthur saw an opportunity to improve the efficiency of his works. He seized it with both hands. He not only modernized Fairfields works at Chepstow (and helped enormously in reorganizing matters at Govan, too), but he built up a reputation for turning out welded girderwork of a quality second to none in the world.

Arthur lived to see welded fabrication work sub-contracted out to Fairfields, Chepstow, by firms with far bigger capacity in their own works in the north-east of England. He saw the first welded bridge trusses on B.R. But he saw only the beginning of the building of the great suspension bridge across the Severn and its smaller brother over the Wye, being done with the help and the skill of the men of his own yard. He died suddenly of a heart attack on 10 December 1964.

Physically, Arthur Nicholas was not a strong man. He put too great a strain on his heart, and that evening he had had to hurry across the "lawn" at Paddington. Although he caught his train, Arthur was dead by the time an ambulance had got him to hospital in Reading; he had collapsed in his seat and the train had made an emergency stop in the vain hope that his life might have been saved. But alas, Arthur had slipped beyond the reach of medical science. It only remained for the melancholy news to be broken to Chris, his devoted wife, who had been preparing his evening meal at their home in Pwll Meyric Lodge.

It was a sad business. Grief lay heavy on the little town of Chepstow. On 14 December, a cold dull winter's day, the Parish Church was packed for the funeral service; the works were closed and silent; even the roar of the traffic which clogged the little winding streets leading up from Rastrick's bridge past the church on its way to the great steelworks in South Wales, was hushed as his friends paid their last respects to Arthur Nicholas, the man who as President of the British Constructional Steelwork Association, had led the country in promoting the use of welding for the fabrication of girder bridges.

British Railways had lost a good friend. The memory of Arthur Nicholas will live long in the Steelwork Office at Paddington. It had been a happy association between railway engineer and steelwork contractor. Patient co-operation had led the way to a fundamental and far-reaching change in the science of making girder bridges. Like in the days of the building of Brunel's bridge over the Wye, history was repeating herself at Chepstow. Once more, the Great Western Railway (disguised under the title of the Western Region of British Railways) was playing a leading role.

The first all-welded (in the shops, the parts were joined together with high strength friction grip bolts in the field) bridge on the W.R. was to span the Holybrook, a few miles west of Reading West Station on the Berks and Hants line. Erected in 1952, it was to set the pattern for many another half-through type plate girder bridge on British Railways. Experience gained led to modifications and improvements in style in later bridges; and eventually, in 1962, it led to the use of the same technique for the modern welded trusses which were to replace Brunel's first "suspension" bridge. The welded Chepstow Bridge spans of 1962 are as much "a first" as was the one which started carrying the broad gauge trains to South Wales in 1852.

CHAPTER 16

Torshear and a Curtain-raiser

THE decision to replace the twin 300-ft truss spans of Chepstow Bridge came in 1960, shortly after an opportunity had been afforded to demonstrate the advantages of welded fabrication in a new 105-ft pony-truss span wanted to carry the High Wycombe to Oxford line over a second carriageway of A40 near Wheatley. The bridge at Wheatley was the guinea-pig; adjoining a riveted span which had been built in 1927, the new and welded span had to have something of the same appearance as the existing riveted truss, it had to be capable of carrying a heavier standard of loading, and quite obviously, it had to embody all the latest improvements affecting future maintenance as well as first cost.

The engineers at Paddington took up the challenge; Fairfields won the contract for the supply and erection of the span at Wheatley, and everything was set for this curtain-raiser to the greater span for Chepstow Bridge. The comparison of statistics shows how welded fabrication helped to lower the weight of steelwork in a span of 111 ft which was to carry a live loading 33 per cent heavier, by 20 per cent less than the riveted bridge. But that was not all. Arthur Nicholas asked permission to assemble and bolt the trusses lying down on their sides so as to avoid having to put up scaffolding for his men to get at the joints in the top chords, as would have been the case in riveting days when trusses had always to be erected in the upright position. The permission was gladly given and the work of bolting was made easier by the introduction of one more innovation, namely the Torshear bolt.

Torshear was the brain-child of the North Bar Tool Company, Bill Brodey's family concern tucked away in a quiet corner of the market town of Banbury. It was a clever idea which took all the responsibility for ensuring that a high-strength friction-grip bolt had been properly tightened away from the man who did the actual screwing up of the nut, and laid it fairly and squarely on the shoulders of the bolt makers and their laboratory metallurgists and inspectors. The idea of Torshear was another stride forward. Another bridge crossed. It meant joints could be correctly bolted up by unskilled labour. The tightening tool, the air-driven wrench, was self-acting too; it needed no great exertion on the part of the operator; it was not a tiring tool to use.

Torshear would not have appeared when it did but for the timely co-operation of father Brodey and his sons Ian and John coming forward to help with the design of a field-joint fastening which was both foolproof and simple to use. The firm had already built up a reputation for producing machine tools to the high standard of quality demanded by Rolls Royce and other makers of aero-engines. The Torshear tool had no reciprocating parts. The drive was through gears worked by a turbine. Once positioned over the end of the bolt and the nut, with the pneumatic supply turned on, Brodey's wrench took a grip of the bolt shank and turned the nut until the end of the shank broke off. This was arranged to happen at a groove specially cut in the threaded portion of the bolt. This groove was located so it would be just a thread-pitch outside the nut after tightening. No Torshear bolt will break off until the nut has been turned sufficiently to exert the required pull in the bolt; the bright shining appearance of the "break" after Torshearing is evidence of the correct grip of this most modern of fastenings.

Of course, the groove must be accurate in shape and size, and the quality and strength of the metal of the bolt has to accord with the narrow limits of a strict specification. So a Torshear bolt does cost a wee bit more than an ordinary one. But the advantages of Torshear far outweigh the extra cost. The tightening is accomplished with so little physical effort that the operator needs only to reach the joint; a ladder will often suffice for he does not have to brace himself against the force of turning the nut, and there is no sudden shock or impact. It is not necessary to hold the head of a Torshear bolt because the whole tightening operation takes place at the nut; a notable convenience when a wall of steel intervenes between the head and the nut, and a fact which makes Torshear the only satisfactory form of countersunk high strength bolt.

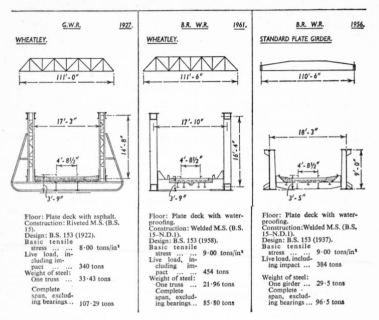

FIG. 13. Table comparing statistics about the truss spans at Wheatley and a standard welded plate girder bridge of similar length.

An inspector looking over a bridge can tell at a glance whether the joints have been correctly tightened. In riveting days, he would have had to climb all over the girderwork, tapping and testing each and every rivet. Today, he has only to run his eye over the sheared-off ends of the bolts.

Torshear, like many another invention, suffered its teething troubles. Ill-treated threads on the bolts, rust and widely differing lubricants, led to variations in tightening in the early days. But, once this foolproof fastener came to be treated with reasonable care, Torshear did in the field what automation had done for welding in the shops.

From the bridge at Wheatley, Torshear spread to many parts. Bolts with the ends of the shanks sheared off were used on the rail-and-road lift bridge at Kingsferry on the Isle of Sheppey, and on the whole of the stiffening trusses of the 1100-ft span of the Tamar Road Bridge. But it was on the new trusses of the Chepstow Bridge that Torshear made its greatest impact. There the bolts were to be of higher ultimate tensile strength than any used elsewhere up to that time; consequently, the numbers of bolts required at each joint were reduced, the cover-plates could be smaller and there were fewer holes to drill.

CHAPTER 17

The First Welded Trusses for a Main Line

JUST as Brunel's trusses at Chepstow had been unique with their single tubular struts, which were really the compression chords of his primitive triangulated girders, so the new 300-ft spans are exceptional in having a single top chord serving two complete truss systems of web members and tension chords. Like the design of 1852, the 1962 idea was unusual. But, whereas Brunel had built his trusses to carry the plate girder railway bridge he hung below them, the bridge of the twentieth century has the ballasted track of the railway on that single-member chord, and there are no cross girders or separate decking. In fact, the new spans have top chords made up out of only five prefabricated boxes.

Here was prefabrication with a vengeance; and, it would never have been possible without the technique of welded design as developed on British Railways since 1948.

At first the members of the Royal Fine Art Commission turned down the idea of substituting deck type spans in place of Brunel's through type spans. The old structure had been classed as an ancient monument, and should be preserved for all time. Besides, they argued, the new span would block out the view downstream seen by people crossing Rastrick's road bridge. However, reason prevailed when it was pointed out that the railway was run for the benefit of the nation to move goods and passengers, and that the cost of interrupting the train service would be far greater if the new spans were to be of the through type, too. No commercial undertaking should be asked to spend an extra £100,000 which is what the new spans would have cost if they had had to be of the through type, just for the sake of sentiment; and as for the view, the bend in the river meant there was nothing to see except a cliff and the buildings of a brush-making factory.

FIGS. 14 & 15. Completely prefabricated on the ground below the "land" spans, the new "river" spans were launched on trollies slung from the underside of Brunel's unique trusses at Chepstow.

The accompanying table of statistics (Fig. 16) comparing the spans of 1852 with those of 1962 shows the amazing reduction in dead weight required in the stronger and more modern superstructures. It also shows something of the work of Frank Leeming, the designer, and his assistants in the Steelwork Office of the Civil Engineering Department of the Western Region; the same thoroughness and attention to detail which characterizes Brunel's plans of the original bridge, is evident in the drawings of the new structure. Indeed, it was thanks to the accuracy of

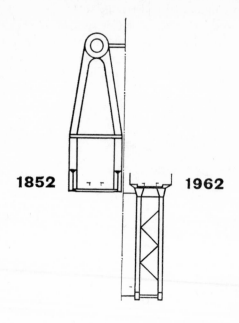

Comparative weights

1852 Wrought Iron Truss:	308 ft. Span	1962 Steel Truss:	300 ft. Span
	Tons		Tons
Tube	138	Complete Truss – Structural Steel	286½
Main Chains	96	Half Weight of Bracing between Trusses	5½
Diagonal Chains	22		
Vertical 'A' Frames	16	*Total Weight of Load Carrying Structure*	292
Track Girders and 'A' Frame Connections	103		
Cross Girders	43	Non-Structural Items: Ballast Plates,	
Total weight of W.I.	418	Parapets, Gutters,	
		Drainage Spigots, etc.	18
Timber Decking (complete)	140	*Total Weight of Steel*	310
Total weight of Load Carrying Structure	558	Ballast	81
		Tiles and Waterproofing	27
Ballast	76	Track	24
Track	24		
Total weight of Structure	658	*Total Weight of Structure*	442
Weight per foot run of load-carrying structure	1.81ton	*Weight per foot run of load-carrying structure*	0.97ton

FIG. 16. The old and the new at Chepstow. One hundred and ten years' progress shows a saving in dead weight of nearly 50 per cent.

designer, fabricator and erector alike that the two "river" spans were reconstructed within the scheduled programme of 14 weeks and without interfering with the train service.

The design and the method of erection of the new trusses as well as the difficult operations of taking away the old "tubular" spans, were all worked out with meticulous attention to detail in the railway engineers' office at Paddington. The contract for the supply and erection of the new work, and the demolition of the old, was arranged with and let to Fairfields. It could hardly have been done otherwise since the site of the bridge adjoined their yard. After all, the firm and its workshops at Chepstow owed their existence to the founding of a works on the site for the very purpose of building Brunel's bridge in 1852. The advantages of an arranged contract were to benefit client and contractor alike, and the whole constructional steelwork industry of the country was to be the better of the advances made in the use of welding in the making of the new spans of this famous bridge.

All the compression members of the new trusses were to be of box-like cross-section. The top chords, 12 ft wide by 3 ft 10 in. deep, were in lengths up to 60 ft and the heaviest parts weighed 34½ tons. The joints between these particular boxes were to be made with internal flanges only, and there were to be no outside cover plates or indeed any bolts on the outside of this chord at all. Now, it so happened that the giant 512 ft long towers of the new Forth Road Bridge were being made in Dalmarnock Iron Works at the time when the specification for the supply of the steelwork for the Chepstow Bridge was being drawn up. One of the more expensive operations was going to be the accurate machining of the internal flanges so that when the whole chord was put together it would have the required camber of 3 in. at the middle of the span, and more important still, be quite straight and true. Arrols had made a wonderful job of the Forth Bridge towers which came out plumb and true to something approaching 1½ in. in the height of over 500 ft. At Chepstow, it was going to be quite a costly business setting up each box to the contractor's one and only large "ending" machine, and then taking it outside the shop to turn it round so the other end could be offered up to the machine. It hardly seemed worth the cost of installing another "ending" machine, and the units were far too large to be turned inside the shop. Whether it was Arthur Nicholas or someone at Paddington who first thought of the idea of giving up all need for machining these important joints, history does not record. Certainly no one hesitated to welcome the suggestion once the *modus operandi* had been explained and understood. The outside surfaces of the internal flanges would be skimmed smooth and made quite true so that when brought into contact as the adjoining boxes were assembled ready for bolting, there would be a perfect bedding together of the surfaces "with no daylight showing between". Apart from that, no elaborate machining operation would be needed. And provided the flanges belonging to the two ends of adjacent boxes were bolted together in perfect contact while the units were being made, they would still give as good a fit when the units were built into the bridge. It was a brilliant bit of thinking on someone's part, and it was to save a lot of money and time. Not that care did not still have to be exercised with the welding of the units because distortion from the heat-input could so easily have spoiled the fit; but that amount of care was much less expensive than the costly machining would have been.

The design made the fullest possible use of prefabrication by automatic welding machines in the shops. The top chords of both the spans contained the two pairs of the top chord plates, and each pair included the gusset plates, butt-welded in the same plane as the chord plates and protruding below them to accommodate the connections to the web members of each truss system. The top plating of the box-section chord was stiffened to form a battle-deck floor which, sloped to drain towards the middle under the railway track and, liberally supplied with drain-pipes passing down right through the chord, was waterproofed and protected with tiles as is the usual practice on British Railway bridges carrying ballasted cross-sleeper tracks. As mentioned already, the ends of the units which made up the top chords were finished with internal flanges. Through these, $2\frac{1}{2}$ in. dowels assured correct alignment. High-strength bolts completed fastenings and took care of stresses caused by the secondary bending of the top chord. The insides of the top chords were ultimately painted, black on the floor and white on the sides and ceiling, and with hinged doors at each end they are accessible for inspection and maintenance. All the other truss members, except the vertical tension hangers which merely support the bottom chords at points midway between the nodal points 60 ft apart, are of box section, unpainted on the insides and completely sealed against the ingress of moisture.

No description of the top chords would be complete without reference to the clever way in which each box unit was put together against its immediate neighbour, and fashioned so that the whole chord when assembled would have the correct amount of camber without having to be strained into shape. Although the way Fairfields went about it was really quite straightforward, it is worthy of study. The first thing was to build a grillage of steel joists on the shop floor. This had to be carefully levelled, and once correct, steps were taken to see that the parts were not likely to get displaced or to settle. This grillage had to be long enough to accommodate two units simultaneously.

The units of the top chord were built in the inverted position, that is to say with the narrower bottom flange uppermost. The chord plates and the gussets which had previously been cut to shape by a gas-burner machine, had already been butt-welded and the welds checked by radiographic examination beforehand. So the four chord plates in each unit were complete before they were set up on the top flange plate (which of course was at the bottom while the unit was upside down) and tack-welded into position. Prefabricated diaphragms kept the chord plates in proper alignment. Next came the steel drainpipes, a line of them straight down the middle of the units, and very useful they proved to be to the platers because not only did each pipe provide a steadying prop when the boxes were closed with the bottom flange plate which was rather wide in its span between the inner chord plates, but they also came in handy for getting hold of the completed units as they were slung from the overhead cranes and moved about the shop.

The platform or grillage on which the units were assembled, two at a time, had been "angled" in the vertical plane. This was to make the whole length of 300 ft of the top chord have a rise or camber of 3 in. upwards at the centre of the span. As one unit neared completion on the assembly platform, the second was built against it, the abutting internal flanges being well pressed together by bolts fully tightened up. Then when the second unit was sufficiently advanced, the first one was lifted away, the second one was moved into the place previously occupied by the first, and the building of the third unit against the other end of the second one went ahead. The other units followed in proper sequence, giving a speedy and businesslike outturn from a well-organized production line.

From this assembly bed, the units progressed to the welding machines for finishing off.

The bottom chord units of the trusses were all box sections, 30 in. deep with the internal width inside kept constant at 18 in. The depth increased to 32 in. at each nodal point. This had been done with a view to improving maintenance conditions during the future life of the bridge; it meant that the top plate had a distinct slope over the whole distance it was between the gusset plates, and the rain water would run off quite freely. We in this country do not have to be worried about mosquitoes breeding in every little puddle left after rain; but, nevertheless, no designer in steelwork likes to see places where water can lodge on his girders. Rust, the enemy, must never be given the chance to gain a foothold.

Technical readers will find interest in another little dodge which went a long way towards keeping the costs of fabrication down. In all the box-section members at least two of the four plates had a thickness not exceeding $\frac{3}{8}$ in.; this meant that the long runs of weld at the four corners of the boxes could be laid down without the need for the edges of the plates to be specially shaped. In other words no edge-preparation was necessary because one of the plates had a thickness of $\frac{3}{8}$ in. or less, and so long as that condition was fulfilled, the deep-penetration welds made a fusion which went the full depth of the thinner of the plates.

The longest prefabricated piece of the bottom chord was 73 ft 2 in. The field joints were in all cases made between the gussets which lay in the plane of the chord plates, and the side plates of the web verticals and diagonals. As well, there were central plates shop-welded between the gussets, to which the web butt-straps were to be bolted when the truss was put together.

In riveting days, the contractor would have been required to put the girderwork together at his works so that the railway company's inspector could check the fit of the various parts and certify that the steelwork had been made well and truly in accordance with the drawings. Not so the welded girderwork for Wheatley and Chepstow. No shop-assembly was called for. This was one more striking economy resulting from the use of modern techniques; and as things turned out the savings were thoroughly justified. At Chepstow, the contractor could have been expected to put things right on site since the work was so to speak just over his garden wall. But the fact is that nothing needed to be put right.

The numbers of high strength bolts required to fasten the parts of the trusses together was only a few hundred; in a riveted bridge of comparable size, the numbers of field bolts to be put in temporarily and taken out again would have run into thousands, and the rivets to be heated, smacked home in the holes and hammered tight would have been numbered in the hundreds of thousands. Scaffolding needed for riveting gangs runs away with a lot of money. Men have got to have something pretty robust to press their weight against as they manipulate the pom-pom air-riveting guns; and that scaffolding has to reach every point where rivets have to be driven, a tall order when girders tower 30 to 40 ft into the air. When it came to bolting together the parts of the welded girders on the river bank, the amount of scaffolding needed was very little indeed.

All the holes had been drilled to their full size before the steelwork left the shop except those in the lower halves of the butt-strap plates fastening the web members to the bottom chord gussets, which had been drilled to a pilot size of only $\frac{9}{16}$ in. This meant that after the trusses had been lined up and checked for camber and straightness, the only site-drilling was the opening out of these holes to the full $\frac{15}{16}$ in. diameter used for the $\frac{7}{8}$ in. bolts; and so far as scaffolding was concerned, none was needed because all these particular holes were at ground level. Nice forward planning.

CHAPTER 18

Chepstow Bridge Reconstruction 1962

(1) THE ERECTION SCHEME AND STRENGTHENING THE CLIFF

LIKE the 1852 spans, the new "river" spans at Chepstow were designed to suit the best way of getting them into position. The 1962 erection scheme benefited from having the old superstructure in place. It could be used to support the new girderwork as it was being launched across the water. But, on the other hand, the bridge was in constant use and the train service should not be interrupted.

By removing the bracings which tied the upstream cylinders to the middle ones at the piers, it was possible to assemble the new Up line span underneath the three 100-ft "land" spans. Then, the new steelwork could be launched; and, after introducing single-line working over the Down line and removing the cross girders and the timber decking of the old Up line span, it could be jacked up in between the wrought iron plate girders of Brunel's bridge and run forward until the Gloucester end came over its new bearings on the cliff. And, finally, the new span would be used as a platform on which the contractor could tackle the difficult problem of taking away the old trusses.

To suit this method of erection, each new span was designed so that it would pass between the cylinders at the piers. This meant that the width of the new girderwork was unusually narrow for a span of 300 ft.

During the launching, each span, 290 tons, was to hang from four cradles slung from 32-wheel trollies moving along runways bolted to the undersides of the 1852 plate girders. Even with the weight, 72½ tons, distributed over a length of 20 ft at each trolly, the loading was going to be too much for the old girders and they had to be given additional support from wire-rope hangers attached to the suspension chains. Apart from this, no other strengthening of the old bridge was necessary.

The new spans were to rest on new concrete bedcourses cast on the virgin rock in the cutting on the Gloucester side. Brunel had built his towers more than 16 ft back from the edge of the cliff; but the bearings of the new spans could not be put so far back from the rockface unless

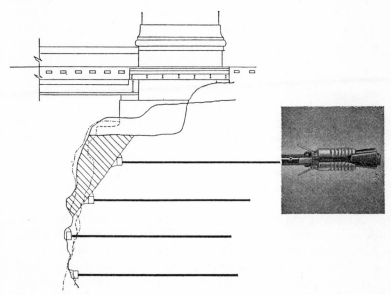

Section under abutment showing anchorage. Note the shaded portion of the rock face which had to be excavated to make way for the girder of the new bridge.

FIG. 17. How the cliff face was strengthened at Chepstow.

a deep trench were excavated in the rock itself; and it would have been rather a waste of money to go cutting away the rock merely to extend the length of girderwork needed to carry the railway over the quarry. That would not have been good engineering. The new spans had been tailored to fit the opening, so now the site had to be made to suit the bridge.

The cliff is an outcrop of carboniferous limestone with the strata dipping down at an angle of 30 degrees from the cliff edge and parallel with the line of the railway. So there was no fear of the upper strata and incidentally the bearings of the bridge, sliding forward over the lower strata and into the river. But there were fissures in the rock. Geologists call them strike planes; they are cracks in the rock running at right angles to the slope of the strata.

To make doubly sure that the bridge was going to be quite safe and that the face of the cliff was not going to suddenly come forward and break off in large chunks, Mark Smith, the Chief Civil Engineer, called in the help of experts. Dr. D. J. Henkel, Ph.D., gave it as his opinion that the falls of rock which had in the past come away from the face of the cliff had occurred as the result of weathering. Apparently, exposure to sun and rain, heat and frost, had led to an opening of the strike plane joints. In the long run, the stability of the cliff face depended upon keeping the effects of the elements at bay. So it was decided to consolidate the cliff in the immediate vicinity of the bedcourses by tying the surface layers tightly back into the heart of the strata where the rock was beyond the reach of the weather. Incidentally, the foundation pressure on the limestone under the new spans was still going to be less than the 11 tons/ft^2 which was the maximum under Brunel's towers.

A contract was let to Rock Mechanics Ltd., who drilled forty holes extending between 30 and 40 ft into the heart of the rock. These holes had a diameter of $1\frac{11}{16}$ in. and lay on a slope of 1 in 12 to the horizontal; they were arranged in four horizontal rows and were spaced 5 ft apart in both directions. Into each hole a Bayliss rock bolt was thrust and then set in a key of concrete. These bolts, $\frac{3}{4}$ in. in diameter and of high tensile steel, were tightened with nuts bearing on steel "washers" 3 in. thick set on 6-in. pads of high quality vibrated concrete. In this way, the cliff face was virtually prestressed, compressed you might say, into the hillside.

Short temporary steel joist spans, spans such as the railways carry in their stocks for emergencies, were inserted over the excavations for the bedcourses. This was routine procedure for carrying the trains over a hole, and the only unusual thing about these temporary works at Chepstow was that they were carried out in bitterly cold weather and in the dead of night, the only time when the traffic people could spare the lines. From the ordinary run of things on the railway when men working on the line seem usually to be called out under conditions of appalling weather, you might say it was not unusual. But the reconstruction of Chepstow Bridge was unusual in that it was a work which had to be undertaken in summer. The line via Gloucester could never be spared during wintertime when every Sunday the direct route to South Wales was closed for routine maintenance work in the Severn Tunnel. So, in one thing at least, the engineers working on the 1962 reconstruction of the Chepstow Bridge were fortunate; they enjoyed the best of the weather. The serious work involving single-line working across the bridge started on 14 July (Bastille Day, by the way) 1962 and the double lines were handed back to the Operating Superintendent on 28 October.

CHAPTER 19

Chepstow Bridge Reconstruction 1962

(2) PREPARATIONS AND LAUNCHING THE NEW SPANS

THE decision to reconstruct the twin "river" spans had been taken towards the end of 1960. The contract for the supply and erection of the new steelwork as well as the demolition of the old superstructures was let to Fairfields on 28 November 1961. Reconstruction of both spans was to be completed before the introduction of the winter time-table in 1962. It was a tight schedule. There were all the calculations to make; 34 sheets of drawings to prepare and the erection scheme to be worked out; and at that time, the rolling mills were refusing to promise to give delivery of the steel within less than nine months from the date of their receiving the order.

The staff of the Steelwork Office in the Civil Engineering Department at Paddington were intensely interested in the work. It was not every day that they were called on to plan the reconstruction of such a large and historic bridge. They were determined to show that the work could be completed on time. Frank Leeming, who was afterwards to fill the post of Assistant Engineer (Bridges) on the Western Region of British Railways, took charge in the design office. It is to his credit and the credit of his team of able draughtsmen that all the drawings were prepared in time and all the drawings of the bridge itself could be used as working drawings by the men on the shop floor. Fairfields did not find it necessary to prepare any supplementary detailing sheets.

The erection scheme also was prepared in the railway bridge engineers' office. It too was, with one exception, to go according to plan; and perhaps that solitary change of plan which concerned the taking down of the tubes might be excused. It was not allowed to prevent the work being finished on schedule.

The story of the erection in 1852 told of the temporary trussing of the tubes with the chains which were eventually to be used as the permanent diagonal braces between the vertical posts in Brunel's spans. The tubes were not strong enough to support their own weight over the whole span length of 300 ft. So, in planning the demolition of the old superstructures in 1962, it was intended to re-use those same diagonal chains to truss the tubes when the heavy suspension chains were being taken away. It was not until the contractor came to try and take down the diagonal chains that it was found the links were rusted together so solidly as to make the joints quite immovable. It was impossible to use those old chains for re-trussing the tubes. This discovery came rather late in the day. The new span had been launched. Work was in full swing and any delay in getting the first tube down was likely to upset the entire programme. Fortunately, as we shall see, some quick thinking produced a workable alternative and the tube was "giggled" down on two towers of trestling ingeniously devised so that they could be dismantled from the bottom upwards.

Iles, the Senior Resident Engineer on the Western Region, took charge of the works on site. Philipson, steelwork inspector on the railway, supervised the fabrication of the new girderwork. Iles had assistance from Horne, a junior resident engineer, and Johnnie Whale from the Steelwork Office helped both in the works and on the site.

We have seen how the new spans were to be erected under the "land" spans. The third of these spans was actually over the water, and it was only at times of exceptionally low tides that one could walk, slither in the mud would be nearer the truth, out to the "river" pier. So the first operation was to build a staging on piles under that "land" span. Fairfields used some old plate girders which had come from the bridge which used to carry the Metropolitan Railway over the main road on the London side of Northwood, to span out to this staging. Actually the Gloucester ends of the new spans were put together first and rolled out on the old Northwood girders to make room for the rest of the steelwork to be built up and bolted, with plant, cranes and so on, operating on the dry ground.

The Up line span being the further from the contractors' works, was the first to be erected. Once the trusses for that span had been completed, there was nothing to prevent progress going ahead with the assembly of the Down line span. And, of course, there was plenty of work that could be gone on with before the working of trains had to be interfered with. One of the benefits of the erection scheme was that the whole of the steelwork for each span except for the handrailing and footpaths on either side of the ballasted railway tracks, could be put together without the need for as much as an hour's occupation of this important trunk route between the Midlands and South Wales.

Another operation which was completed while the trains were still using both lines across the bridge, was the erection of the runways from which the new spans were to be slung while being launched out over the river. These consisted of new steel joists 24 in. deep, held in position against blocks of wood between their top flanges and the bottoms of Brunel's plate girders. They were supported entirely with hook bolts which passed through holes in the said plate girders; this arrangement meant that these valuable new joists did not have to be spoiled by drilling, and they remained "as new" and ready to be credited for and taken into the railway's stock of emergency plant. The runways had to be level. The bridge had a slope of 1 in 200 up towards the cliff. Hence the blocks of wood against which the runway joists were bolted. These timber packings were of varying thickness so that the joists could be level, and the 290 tons of new steelwork, the weight included the usual clubber associated with steelwork erectors, did not have to be launched up hill.

Single-line working was introduced after the last train crossed the Up line on Saturday 14 July. John Bickerton, the District Engineer at Newport in whose section the bridge lay, was there to see the train go across. It was a parcels train worked by a Bo-Bo diesel-electric locomotive, and John recalls how the quietness of the country night was broken by a succession of "last posts" blown by the driver on the horn of the locomotive.

As the sounds of the horn died away the permanent way men stood ready to start their part in the reconstruction of these historic spans; and, as soon as the train had cleared the section, they moved in to remove the rails and sleepers and shovel away the hundreds of tons of ballast. They, too, had been mechanized since Brunel's day; the ballast was swept up by mechanical shovels running not on the rails but crawling about first on the stones of the ballast and later on the close-boarded timber deck of the old span.

There were other strange things to be seen on the railway line that Sunday. Fairfields sent two mobile road cranes to work on the old span, a 6-tonner and one which could lift 25 tons; and the only way these machines could reach the bridge was via the goods yard at Chepstow station, and along the quarter of a mile of track which incidentally included ducking their jibs under the station footbridge. The cranes had to help each other in passing under that bridge, the lighter one going first and then swinging round to take the weight of the heavier one's jib as it wriggled its way over the sleepers and ballast. Permanent way does not make a good track for a vehicle running on road wheels, and such were the shakings and shudderings of those two cranes that everyone, not least their drivers, sighed with relief when they finally made the journey none the worse for their buffeting.

On Monday 16 July, the day set for the launching of the Up line span, there was quite an air of expectancy at the bridge. Photographers, several of the technical staff from the Paddington offices including Ted Outram who was in overall charge of the Steelwork Office design section, and Reggie Stone, who ruled over the section engaged in examining and reporting on the state of corroding girderwork throughout the Western Region, Frank Leeming and others had come to see the critical operation. It was known the old wrought iron girders were going to have to carry a load more concentrated than was their habit, and experts were stationed on those girders to watch and see, just in case anything looked like going amiss. In fact, one panel of the upstream girder was found to be developing a buckle. This amounted to a bulge of half an inch, and there was an anxious moment just while the heavy load passed; but in a web plate 84 in. deep, it was not serious and when relieved of the load, the plate went straight again. Insignificant as this distortion was, it did confirm the belief that it was high time the bridge was reconstructed. Perhaps, like the "land" spans in 1944, the factor of safety was nearing unity.

George Davies, Fairfield's Outdoor Manager, was Arthur Nicholas's agent on the work. And when he and Iles agreed that all was in readiness for the launch to begin, the chocks were taken away and the 290 tons of new steelwork started to roll forward on the first 270 ft of its journey. It was a rather grey chilly day for July. Not that one had time to look at anything besides the work in hand; but, afterwards, I remember being pleased it had not turned out wet. The photographers, headed by Bill Macdonald from Paddington, got a good record of the operation. Later for the benefit of cinema audiences they speeded up the movement.

At the tail, the new span rested on hard steel balls, 3 in. in diameter, running along tracks formed by laying bull-headed rails on their sides. At the nose, the span hung from cradles slung below the two runways and running on 64 wheels. The "push" required to move the 290 tons, came from a small winch. The greatest effort, which was at starting from rest, did not have to exceed $2\frac{1}{2}$ tons; the theorists had predicted the force would be one-eleventh of 10 per cent of the weight to be moved, or just over 2·6 tons. Practice was proving they were right.

The span could not go all the way because in its initial launching level, the nose would have hit the cliff at a point somewhere below the bedcourse. It had had to be started off at a level well below the underside of the decking of the old span. Before it could be raised to an inch or so above its final level, the timber decking of the old span had to be taken away and room made for the new steelwork to be jacked up in between the wrought iron girders which carried the runways from which the travelling cradles were slung. So there had to be a pause in its travels while two different sets of cradles were brought into use on the runways, and the whole weight transferred to Brunel's span.

At the beginning, the new span had been supported from below at the tail and slung from above at the nose. Both these points of support had been equidistant from the centre of the mass being moved. For jacking it higher and for travelling the last 30 ft or so, it was to be slung from two different sets of cradles. Again, these points of support were to be equidistant from the middle. This was done to ensure the loads on the runways would be the same at each of the four cradles. Also, by this arrangement, the runways did not have to extend beyond the second verticals in Brunel's trusses; and the expense of fitting auxiliary hangers to give intermediate support to the Gloucester-end span of the wrought iron plate girders was avoided.

CHAPTER 20

Chepstow Bridge Reconstruction 1962

(3) RAISING AND LANDING THE NEW SPANS AND TAKING AWAY THE OLD TRUSSES

REMOVING the timber decking and the cross girders from between the plate girders of the old span did not take long. The road cranes lifted the parts away as quickly as the ironwork could be cut through with oxy-acetylene torches. By Sunday 22 July, the way was clear for the new span to be raised up and travelled forward on to the cliff. I remember that warm summer day. There were a few workmen on the site. The sixteen 25-ton Hydralite jacks were in position on the cradles. All was in readiness for the lift to start early on the Monday morning.

There was a friendly atmosphere about the work at Chepstow. Nevertheless, if George Davies could get ahead while Iles or his assistants were not looking, he liked to do so. It was only natural. No one likes being watched while they are feeling their way with something they have not done before. Now, Iles lived at Bristol and normally he did not reach Chepstow until half past nine on a Monday morning. So when I visited the bridge after breakfasting at the George Hotel on that fateful Monday morning, I was surprised to find a site strangely silent. The place seemed deserted. The span still hung at its original level.

Arthur Nicholas was away on business and was not expected back until after midday. In the main offices of Fairfields, I found George Davies and his foremen. Iles was there, too. All seemed depressed. "We've been trying to raise her since early dawn," they said. "She simply won't budge. The jacks seem to be overloaded and we've had to send two into the machine shop for stripping down and fitting new leathers." It was a depressing situation. All hope that the lift would be well under way by the time Arthur Nicholas turned up, faded.

Now, there is protocol about procedure on a site where a Resident Engineer is holding a watching brief over a contractor. In this case, Iles was in charge. The Bridge Assistant was there solely in the capacity of adviser. It was not that everyone was not desperately keen to see the job going on. No one could have been more keen than George Davies and Iles; but jacking up a big weight that is hanging on a rather groggy old structure is an operation in which one cannot afford to take the slightest risk. The bursting of a jack could cause an overloading of the others; the sudden dropping of 290 tons through even a fraction of an inch could have had catastrophic results.

The sixteen 25-ton jacks should have been ample for the job. There seemed to be a good margin. The whole span after completion was not going to weigh more than 310 tons. Surely, a jacking capacity of 400 tons was more than adequate. Had someone made an error? Perhaps the weight of contractor's clubber was more than we thought. Anyway, after a discussion round the table, it was agreed to have another try and off we all trooped back to the bridge and to the jacking platforms.

Now, the actual jacking took place round four verticals on the new trusses, the arrangement being that the new work climbed up giant steel flats hanging from the cradles. To begin with the weight rested on giant-sized steel pins passing through holes in the flats and resting on saddles. There were a succession of these holes in the flats and they were spaced at intervals corresponding to slightly less than the full stroke of the jacks. A second set of pins transferred the weight to the next holes in the flats after the jacks had raised the load through 10 in. The jacks had a stroke of 12 in., and the total lift was between 7 and 8 ft. So the men, one to each jack, had a long haul in front of them. In fact, each man was going to lift a little over 18 tons through a height of more than 7 feet; that they succeeded in doing this in 3½ days for the first span and cutting the time to less than one whole day for the second, showed just what could be done when once they had got into the hang of things. But to return to that fateful first attempt on the Monday morning. The second try got no further than the first. There were four jacks to each vertical and it was essential to keep the rate of lift the same at each jack. Careful check was kept on the extensions of

PLATE 23. The buckled web plate in the "land" spans of Chepstow Bridge on 4 April 1944. (Photo: B.R.)

PLATE 24. The split in the web plate of the middle girder of the bridge near Weston Rhyn. (Photo: B.R.)

PLATE 25. Tightening Torshear bolts in the web joint of a 200-ft long welded plate girder of a railway bridge at Danygraig near Swansea. Starting near the middle, the operator works outwards tightening all the bolts before returning again to the centre and giving the final "Torshearing" which breaks off the surplus shank.

PLATE 26. Erecting the prefabricated floor units of a half-through type welded girder bridge on the Western Region of British Railways.

PLATE 27. The bridge over the A40 near Wheatley. The 1927 riveted span is on the left.

the rams; measurements were taken as the rams rose, $\frac{1}{16}$ in. by $\frac{1}{16}$ in., and the safety nuts were screwed down—the safeguard against a jack losing its load through failure of the hydraulic system; but it was all to no avail. It seemed impossible for all sixteen men and their jacks to keep in unison. Time and again, individual jacks would jam. Apparently, the overloading of some jacks when others lagged behind was too much for them. Defeated, a somewhat dejected party returned to the works to await Arthur's arrival.

After lunch, another discussion. Then a phone call to the engineers at Tangye's, the suppliers of the jacks, and a promise of another sixteen jacks, this time of 50-ton capacity to make sure, being sent down by road from Birmingham on the morrow. So there was nothing else to be done about lifting the new span until the jacks arrived. The men were given other jobs to be getting on with.

The change to the jacks of larger capacity did the trick, however; and with the bigger margin, the lift went ahead without hitch, the span was rolled forward and set down on its bearings by the following Saturday afternoon. It had been launched with most of the steelwork for making the connections to the pier cylinders already in position at the tail end. Steel bands had been clamped round the cylinders and were further secured against any chance of slipping by steel set screws in holes drilled through and tapped in the steel of the bands and the $1\frac{1}{4}$ inch thick wall of the cast iron cylinders.

On Sunday 29 July, a party of consulting engineers from London came down to have a look at the job. One felt relieved to know the new span was safe and sound on its permanent bearings before the visitors arrived. One of them, Peter Stott, was to become Chief Engineer to the Greater London Council within a couple of years. And on 2 August the work was visited by Mark Smith, Chief Civil Engineer, who brought Stanley Raymond, the General Manager of the W. Region, along too. In the New Year's honours list in 1967, Mr. Raymond was to become Sir Stanley.

There is something very stimulating about showing one's work to eminent visitors. Perhaps it is a pride in the job; I prefer to think it is a feeling of pride in one's association with a magnificent band of helpers. No one man plans or carries through a single large civil engineering work; it would never be started let alone finished without the patient willing co-operation of every worker, be he draughtsman, crane-driver, welder or tea-boy; and at Chepstow it was like one great party.

Having got the first span into position, attention was turned to the hardly less difficult business of getting the old wrought iron truss down. Once the plate girders no longer had to carry heavy concentrated loads, the diagonal bracing chains could be unfastened and used to truss the tube while the main "suspension" chains were destressed. At least that had been the plan, following, in reverse, Brunel's erection scheme of 1852. But no one had bargained for the state of the joints in those diagonal chains; the ravages of rust during 110 years' exposure had "welded" the links together at each pinned joint, and it proved quite impossible to make use of those chains. Various other ways were considered for trussing the tube and making it self-supporting over the length of 300 ft; but each idea involved delay. Delay while some piece of equipment was fetched from the other end of the country. Already time was running out, the work was getting behind schedule, and three days had been lost over the jacking troubles. Besides, the work had been authorized against the expenditure of a certain sum of money, and additional charges could not be incurred.

It is a bad thing to leave the crossing of one's bridges until one reaches them. Forward planning is essential if a job is to progress on the right lines. Here indeed was a black mark against the Bridge Assistant's record. He should have known better than to trust to those chains. Perhaps.

The tube continued to stay where it was for another couple of days and then George Davies and Arthur Nicholas came along with the idea of "giggling" the tube down on two bents of military trestling. Here was the answer. There was an ample quantity of the trestling belonging to the railway and actually lying in Chepstow. At least most of it. Why on earth had not the idea of using it occurred to any one before.

The towers of this trestling were to be built up alongside the struts, or as we came to call them, the A-frames (because of their shape) of Brunel's truss, and then with the heavy slings and gallows-beam arrangements already devised and in position over each end of the tube, the 138-ton pipe was to be lowered step by step while supported first on one tower of trestling and then on the other, until it could be landed on railway trucks and wheeled off the bridge for cutting up and removal by road. Even now, the idea was not so simple as it sounded, the towers of trestling were going to be very awkward to take down from the *top* while the tube was still on the towers. The pieces of the trestling were too heavy to be man-handled, they needed cranes to lift the parts, and the tops of the towers were out of reach of any crane. It was at this stage that Ted Outram came forward with his idea of doing the job upside down. By fastening the tops of the trestling towers to the tube, each could be made to hang from the tube and it could be dismantled piece by piece from the bottom upwards.

When Brunel had built the tubes, had he fashioned them to the vertical curve with the rise of 30 in. at the centre? Or had he made them quite straight and bent them afterwards? On the drawings showing how the tubes were to be moved to their position at right angles to the river bank, they appeared to be quite straight before being trussed for launching. So it was assumed the bow was put into them after fabrication. No doubt, Brunel had aimed at making the bridge trusses nice and tight to prevent the chains dancing about under the passage of trains. It was not unlike the principle of the bow-and-string in his 200-ft bow-string trusses across the Thames at Windsor. All the same, it must have taken a considerable force to bend the Chepstow tubes; and, in working out the scheme for destressing the chains prior to cutting them, there was some speculation as to how much force the A-frames were exerting on the chains. It mattered because that force would have to be "let go" gently and slowly; it would not be safe to cut through links carrying a "tightness" of a hundred tons or more, and let the ends go suddenly.

Subsequently, it seemed certain the tubes must have been built straight and curved from end to end afterwards. Nevertheless, such a method made the Chepstow tubes unique. At Saltash, the tubes look from a distance as though they are curved from end to end, but actually they were built as a succession of chords, kinked at each nodal point. The Forth Bridge tubes likewise are straight between the points of intersection; it is much easier to make a tube straight than build it with a "vertical" curve.

Once the road cranes had worked their way on to the deck of the new span, steps were taken to cut and remove the end sections of the wrought iron plate girders. The diagonal chains followed, being burned through and taken away in sizeable pieces by the cranes. Next, needle-beams were slipped through holes cut in the web plates of the middle sections of the girders, and the weight of these pieces supported on the deck of the new span. This was necessary because once the main chains were destressed and made ready for lifting off, there would be nothing left to carry these 140-ft long girders.

Dove-tailed into this complicated programme came the laying of the rails and sleepers of the permanent way so as to be ready for the railway wagons to be run into position to receive the tube. Careful planning was necessary to make sure the road-cranes did not get hemmed in by the towers of trestling, the railway line, the needle-beams and so forth. At last, with the trestle towers completed, destressing day arrived. For this operation, brackets were bolted on to the A-frames, and windows burned out of the web plates. There were two of these stout steel brackets on each side of the web, and they were about 3 ft 6 in. apart. Between the upper and lower brackets, four 25-ton hydraulic jacks, each with a pressure gauge, were pumped up to press hard on the brackets, and the last remaining parts of the A-frame struts, the flanges, were cut through. Then, with the full "bow-and-string" force transferred to the jacks, it was a simple matter to read the loading on the gauges—it was found to be about 54 tons at each A-frame—gently release the valves in the jacks, and let the main suspension chains hang free.

There followed the cutting up of these heavy chains; their removal along with the middle lengths of the plate girders, and the lowering of the tube.

The tube was cut through just clear of the permanent towers of the old bridge. Fairfields had erected a Scotch derrick on the cliff top above the cutting on the Gloucestershire bank, and a light tall tower crane, capable of dealing with 3 tons when the wind was not blowing faster than 40 miles an hour, on the ground at the Chepstow end of the bridge. The former lifted away the tube in convenient lengths after it had been withdrawn into the cutting, and also dealt with all the lifts needed in connection with the part of the tube left behind on the masonry portal towers. Via a road track temporarily cut along the top of the hillside above the cutting, lorries carted the scrap pieces of tube round by Rastrick's old bridge over the Wye and so to Fairfields' yard.

The actual dismantling of the portal towers could not be allowed to proceed until the Down line truss of Brunel's old bridge had been removed. But once the right-away was given, it took little time to lower away the cast iron plate work of the Chepstow tower; and it was there that the maker's name—IRISH ENGINEERING COMPANY, SEVILLE IRON-WORKS, DUBLIN—came to light.

The removal of the masonry portals at the Gloucester end presented a much more difficult problem. They were found to consist of pennant stone blocks keyed and clamped together with wrought iron bars run in with lead. The core was hard sound brickwork. It seemed a shame to be having to take down such fine masonry work; but, of course, the orders had been agreed and the whole of the towers had to come down and be removed. Actually, in spite of having been built in the days of the broad-gauge, the insides of the towers had infringed the statutory dimensions of the 4 ft $8\frac{1}{2}$ in. gauge railway structure gauge.

CHAPTER 21

Safety Assured

ANY new idea in structural design, be it in the frame of an aeroplane or the girderwork of a bridge, calls for scientific test and analysis. Chepstow Bridge was no exception. So much of the design and the method of manufacture were novel. For length and carrying capacity, the new 300-ft spans contained less steel than any comparable railway bridge in the world.

The erection procedure had called for the use temporarily of one new span—the Up one—alone by trains before it could be given the lateral support afforded by the bracing which was eventually to link both Up and Down spans together. Used alone like this, the Up span had a width of only 12 ft; without the permanent handrailing and footpath, the width of the steelwork was only one-twenty-fifth of the span length. This ratio was unusually small. From experience with riveted steelwork, the lateral oscillation under the passage of trains might have been expected to be alarmingly high.

So the appearance of three heavy mineral locomotives working back from Swindon works to South Wales on the Sunday morning after the Up span had been brought into use, was especially welcome. Due warning of the working of these engines had been received from "Control", and permission was given to make what use the engineers liked of them for testing the bridge so long as the occupation of the line did not exceed half an hour.

There was no time to set up strain-gauges; only pencil-and-card apparatus would be available. It was all that was needed to record the movement of the middle of the new span; the old span alongside afforded the "datum". By fixing a wooden board on the old span so that it stood vertical and at right-angles to the railway track, a stiff cardboard pinned to it would be held steady while a pencil clamped to a metal spring projecting from the new span would follow the movements of the new span and trace a record of those movements on the cardboard.

The engines, coupled together, made three runs across the bridge. In the fastest, 25 miles an hour, the maximum then possible because of the restrictive curvature at the approaches to the bridge while the temporary single-line working was in force, a deflection of 1·6 in. was recorded. This was very satisfactory, the figure was considerably less than might have been expected from these three heavy locomotives. But it was not the figure the engineers were most concerned about. No one doubted the strength of the span to resist vertical bending; it was the amount of sideways shake the slender steelwork was going to experience before it was fastened to its twin span alongside that really mattered. The pencil line showed the greatest lateral displacement did not exceed 0·20 in. This was highly satisfactory. It meant that no further restriction below the speed permitted in the interests of the safety of the men working on the bridge need be enforced.

Single-line working had lasted from 14 July until 28 October 1962 when both new spans were brought into use. Official tests were carried out on 5 and 6 November when royalty in the persons of "King Henry VI" and "King James I" spent two murky (and most unphotogenic) days thundering back and forth over the Up span. The test train consisted of these two "King" class engines hauling loaded ballast trucks in a train long enough to cover the 300 ft span. Crossings were made at speeds varying between a dead slow crawl and 35 miles an hour, in an effort to determine if there was any speed intermediate between these limits at which the vibrations in the girderwork were likely to synchronize with the impact effects caused by the engines themselves and the wheels of the train thumping over the rail-joints. The testers would have preferred to have had some less well-balanced engines than the 4-cylinder "Kings"; but it was a case of having to be content with what one was given, and after all, the "King" had as heavy a static axle-load as any locomotive then operating over the Western Region.

A study of the continuous records of electric resistance strain-gauge readings taken at different parts of the structure confirmed the accuracy of the designers' calculations. There appeared to be no critical speed within the range. The span could not be made to "resonate" during these test runs; and as a sharp curve in the permanent alignment of the railway between the bridge and Chepstow station prevents trains from crossing the bridge at higher speeds, it was pointless to pursue the matter any further.

Chepstow Bridge was reconstructed because some parts of the wrought ironwork were being stressed beyond the endurance limit, and, in consequence, the iron could not be expected to withstand an indefinite number of repetitions of such loading. This does not mean the superstructure had reached a state in which it was about to collapse; and it would be quite wrong to say the metal had become fatigued. Indeed, no bridge has been known to fail solely through metal-fatigue.

It used to be supposed that vibration caused a change to take place in the structure of the metal itself, making the material brittle. This apparently led to the term metal-fatigue. It was also supposed that in the course of time wrought iron changed its texture, and thereby its strength, under the effects of age. Temperature changes throughout the year, the ranges of cyclic loading, and what was referred to as recovery time during the intervals between the applications of loading, were all suspected of altering the substance of the metal. At Chepstow the repetitions of loading on some parts of the iron were known to have exceeded two million; the wrought ironwork had stood through the winters and summers of 110 years; the loadings had varied through a wide range; and the intervals of time between applications might have had some effect on the so-called recovery. Here was an opportunity of carrying out tests which could never be faithfully copied in a laboratory; a chance to see if the metal had deteriorated through the passage of time, and in particular whether there had been any lowering of the limit of endurance.

Specimens of the wrought iron were cut from places in the bridge. Some had been subjected to more than two million cycles of loading and the range of stress had varied from a pull of $2 \cdot 9$ tons/in^2 to a pull of $4 \cdot 4$; others which had endured the same number of cycles of loading had been alternately pulled with a tensile stress of $1 \cdot 0$ tons/in^2 and pushed with a compressive stress of $3 \cdot 6$; while others of exactly the same vintage had come from places where they had carried no stress whatsoever. All were tested in the Western Region laboratory at

Swindon where they were subjected to cycles of the same range of loading. In his report the metallurgist wrote: "There is no significant variation in the remaining fatigue life of the wrought iron due to its previous condition of loading." The endurance limit remained unchanged.

Providentially for bridge engineers the endurance limit, the stress below which wrought iron and mild steel can be subjected to unlimited repetitions of loading without fear of fracture, is about 50 per cent of the ultimate breaking stress; and since the allowable working stress is less than 30 per cent of the ultimate breaking stress, bridges are unlikely to suffer from metal-fatigue.

Why then, it might be argued, is it necessary to reconstruct bridges? The answer is really very simple. It is just a matter of the metal being overstrained through overstress brought about through overloading. Neglecting any reduction in the volume of the metal through corrosion, the overloading will have been caused either by putting too much load on (the method of applying the load matters, too, since a light weight applied suddenly can give the effect of a heavy load) or by defects in design such as occur at a point of discontinuity in the metal like a sharp corner, a hole or an indentation, and result in a concentration of stress.

At Chepstow the old spans suffered a combination of loading heavier than Brunel had envisaged, and a design that had many places of high concentration of stress. In some parts the wrought iron had been overstrained. The area affected was very small; but in the course of time the effects were to gradually spread (Chapter 1) and weaken the whole structure.

The overstressing which caused the overstraining was confined to the track girders and the A-frames. The bridge was certainly not reaching the state of being in imminent danger of collapse. Neither was it suffering from metal-fatigue, as engineers would define the term; but there was evidence of corrosion-fatigue.

Corrosion-fatigue is a different complaint altogether; it must not be confused with metal-fatigue. Corrosion-fatigue is a very real danger in neglected steelwork (and wrought ironwork, too). It is simply a rusting of the surface of the steel so that the layer next to the surface loses its strength. For a while the rusted layer stays on, holding moisture and generally encouraging further rusting. The next layer of steel, as yet unaffected by rust, gradually becomes more and more highly stressed until it, too, enters the state of no-return; the rust drops off; the process eats further into the good metal, until eventually the girder loses its shape, develops a sag, and shows evidence of weakness. This is failure through corrosion-fatigue, but it is not metal-fatigue.

Now all sorts of things can raise the working-stress beyond the limits which the designer intended. That is why, in the past, bridges have tended to wear out. Rusting and the loss of metal are obvious. To prevent these steelwork has to be painted. Even if it is protected by a sacrificial coating of a non-ferrous metal such as aluminium or zinc, the surface has still to be painted periodically if its life is to be prolonged.

What is not so obvious, is the raising of the stress by some interruption or obstacle to the "flow" of the lines of the principal stresses. Theoretically, the net area of a section across a bar of steel with a hole in it may be ample to carry a certain load; but the congestion of the lines of stress, interrupted in their smooth path along the bar, is sometimes enough to multiply the intensity of stress threefold where they squeeze past the hole. Again, the same sort of thing happens if a plate is fastened to a bar with a fillet weld running at right angles to the lines of principal stress. The stress has to "bob down" under the "upset metal" at the weld, and once more a congestion gives rise to an increase in the intensity of stress.

CHAPTER 22

Post Mortem

NONE of the bridge failures described in this book can be rightly attributed to metal-fatigue. The fractures in the cast iron beams were, in every case, caused through overloading the metal. At the Dee Bridge, Robert Stephenson made a mistake by "prestressing" the end piece of the compound beam with wrought iron bars placed so high up in the depth of the girder that their presence had the effect of increasing the tensile forces in the bottom flange. At Inverythan and Norwood Junction there were hidden flaws in the tension flanges of the cast iron beams. The "high" girder spans of the first Tay Bridge were blown over because Bouch had not taken proper account of the forces of the wind in his design, and he had not bothered to keep a proper check on the manufacture of the cast iron components of his spindly trestles on the piers.

The girder of the "land" spans of Brunel's Chepstow Bridge buckled because the web plate had not been stiffened sufficiently to enable the bridge to carry locomotives and trains which were far heavier than had been envisaged at the time of construction ninety-two years before. Corrosion-fatigue was the cause of the splitting of the middle girder at Weston Rhyn, and of the breaking of the centre hangers below the "suspension" trusses of the Royal Albert Bridge; at both, failure had followed accumulative weakening by the rusting away of the metal at inaccessible places.

Why then, had not the failures occurred sooner?

The Dee bridge had given trouble; the truss-bars had been tightened, making matters worse, and collapse had come within months of the opening of the line. But at Inverythan and Norwood Junction the bridges had been in use twenty-five and thirty-one years respectively before they suddenly gave way. The cast iron in the vicinity of the flaws must have been highly stressed from the day the girders were brought into use. The margin of safety must have been narrow from the very start. Some slight change in loading, perhaps some small re-distribution in the permanent way, was all that was needed to break the beams. Being of cast iron, brittle and lacking the ductility of a girder made of a wrought ferrous metal, failure came suddenly and without warning. A wrought iron or mild steel girder would have distorted gradually, perhaps taking many weeks to show signs of a loss of camber, and the bridge would have shown evidence of weakening which a vigilant bridge inspector would have been quick to spot. A cast iron girder bridge, on the other hand, would be unlikely to give any indication of impending collapse; at the best, there might be some loosening of the bolts holding the cross-timbers to the cast iron, which might have roused suspicions of some redistribution of loading; but with the real defects hidden inside the cast iron, there was really nothing to indicate the bridge was about to give way.

In contrast, the partial failure of the main girder in the Chepstow "land" span did not result in a catastrophe. The wrought iron web plate did tear away from the bottom flange, partly splitting and partly shearing at the rivets; but the bridge did not fall down. The wrought iron gave ample warning that something was wrong.

The mishap at Chepstow Bridge, instead of being a black mark against Brunel, had shown the skill of an engineer who was master of his trade. Brunel had been building the railway to carry trains which had a loading equivalent to about one and a quarter tons on every foot of track. The shareholders of those days would not have been pleased to see money squandered on structures strong enough to carry trains of twice that weight; it would have been no credit to Brunel if he had made the bridges unnecessarily strong. He had established by actual test that the bridge would safely bear a uniformly distributed weight of $2\frac{1}{2}$ tons per foot run; but that was in a single application; it had been a test load of 770 tons put on but once to show that under the normal traffic for which the bridge had been designed there was a proper margin of safety. The builder of a bridge constructed in 1852 should not be accused of failing in his duty if, more than ninety years later, the structure should prove incapable of carrying trains twice as heavy as those for which it was designed.

The determination of the stress in the girder of a bridge is by no means easy; the problem is beset by many indeterminables. To begin with, all that can be measured is the change in strain caused by running a load across the bridge. The stress caused by the dead weight of the structure itself can be found only through calculation; those stresses which may have been built into the parts of a girder when it was being made at the works or perhaps when the members were being forced and strained into position during erection in the bridge, remain unknown.

The actual measurement of the change of stress under trains, be they special test engines and trains or the normal service, has been brought to an advanced state of scientific refinement, and the stresses, in terms of tons per square inch, can be computed to an accuracy equivalent to the second place of decimals. This is achieved through sticking an electric-resistance strain gauge against the surface of the iron or steel and passing an electric current through the wire. In the circuit there is a galvano-meter which is used to measure the changes in the flow of current; the electrical resistance of the gauge alters as the gauge is stretched or shortened in sympathy with the surface of the metal to which it is stuck; and it is the effect of this change of resistance to the flow of the current which is measured and recorded.

Nevertheless, no matter how accurately these changes of stress may be determined, there still remain many imponderables when it comes to a matter of assessing the variations in the loading effect imposed on the structure by the motion of engines and trains on the permanent way.

When "Locomotion" and her sisters "Hope", "Black Diamond" and "Diligence" trundled along the Stockton & Darlington Railway, the men who rode on these first engines of the world's first public railway were very sensitive to the up-and-down heaving of the whole contraptions as the vertical pistons moved up and down. On the Liverpool & Manchester Railway opened in 1830, George Stephenson was to feel the effects of a similar though more severe motion on his immortal "Rocket". "Locomotion" had, and indeed still has for she has been preserved and today stands honoured in Darlington station, her two cylinders located on the centre-line of the boiler, and as a runner she must have been pretty steady and without any tendency to "nose" her way along the track with wheel flanges bearing first against one rail and then against the other. Perhaps that was just a happy fluke; for as soon as George put the cylinders on the slope and one each side as he did on the "Rocket", he started to run into real trouble. At first, while the cylinders were inclined at 45 degrees, the motion was quite alarming; in the Rainhill Trials, the "Rocket", averaging nearly 14 miles an hour over a total distance of 60 miles, literally shouldered her way to victory as she lurched and "nosed" from side to side along the track. It was not to be long before George had the cylinders brought down to as nearly horizontal as he could get them; and when his 2-2-0 "Planet" appeared in 1830 her pair of cylinders were placed horizontal and between the frames at the leading end.

Some notice was being taken of the meaning of Newton's third law: to every action there is an equal and opposite reaction. But many years were to pass before serious efforts were to be made to assess the effects of the out-of-balance couples exerted by locomotives on bridges.

For close on a hundred years bridge engineers put up with the unfortunate behaviour of the steam locomotive. The factor of safety gave margin enough. But as axle-loads started to rise in an attempt to make engines pull heavier and faster trains at a time when the railways of this country were beginning to feel the effects of competition from the roads, it was a case of either strengthening existing bridges or allowing higher permissible stresses. Wholesale reconstruction of hundreds of bridges would have meant a complete dislocation of traffic; wholesale strengthening would have incurred heavy expenditure; almost in desperation, the bridge engineers were forced to see if after all something could be got out of the factor of safety. Was the margin of safety extravagantly wide? There seemed good reason to suspect greater loads could be carried over the bridges without imperilling the trains.

There is a story related by Sir Felix Pole in his memoirs. Collett had just produced his "Caerphilly Castle" which created enormous interest in railway and allied circles in 1923. It was announced as being pre-eminent as the most powerful passenger train engine in the country. Its tractive effort was 31,625 lb, as compared with the then most powerful Gresley "Pacific", whose tractive effort was less than 30,000 lb. One

of the directors of the Great Western Railway was Sir Aubrey Brocklebank, whose knowledge of locomotive practice was considerable. Sir Aubrey pointed out to Sir Felix Pole that in some ways the "Castle" class were not entirely satisfactory. Probably Sir Aubrey had in mind the Paddington to Birmingham run where the heavy two-hour trains were proving rather too much for a single "Castle". In due course, when talking over locomotive matters with Collett, Sir Felix says the question of axle-loading came up. At the time the maximum permissible axle load was 19½ tons, and full advantage had been taken of this in designing "Caerphilly Castle". Collett lamented the fact that compared with axle loading in America British locomotive practice was badly hampered, and remarked: "If I could have an axle load of 22½ tons, I would give you a very fine locomotive." At a subsequent chat with Sir Aubrey the latter asked what was in fact the real carrying capacity of the main line. The Chief Engineer was called in and asked for what axle load did he provide when designing new bridges. His reply was 22 tons. This seems to have taken the General Manager by surprise. Sir Felix writes that he and Sir Aubrey were astonished, "especially when it transpired that it had been standard practice for over twenty-two years," since the days when Sir James Inglis was chief engineer of the G.W.R. On enquiry, Sir Felix continues, the original calculation had "a sufficient factor of safety to permit 22½-ton axle loading".

A committee of enquiry set up in 1923 was the first really serious attempt "to conduct researches with reference to the stresses in Railway Bridges, especially as regards the effects of moving loads". It was the modern counterpart of the 1847 Enquiry set up after the Dee bridge disaster. But this time no unfortunate mishap had been the cause for setting up a top-level committee; the 1923 Bridge Stress Committee were to see if it were possible through being better acquainted with the loadings, to be more precise about the safe load-carrying capacity of Britain's railway bridges. They sought to find out what allowance should be made for "stress due to impact". This they defined as being any stress which a load causes by reason of its own motion or the motion of its parts; they were careful to point out that the name of impact effect was usual and convenient though scarcely logical.

The Bridge Stress Committee appointed in March 1923 had the following membership:

Sir J. Alfred Ewing, K.C.B., F.R.S., M.Inst.C.E. (Chairman)

C. J. Brown, C.B.E., M.Inst.C.E. (L. & N.E.R.)
A. C. Cookson, M.Inst.C.E., F.C.G.I. (G.W.R.)
Professor W. E. Dalby, F.R.S., M.Inst.C.E.
G. Ellson, O.B.E., M.Inst.C.E. (Southern Railway)
Sir Robert Gales, M.Inst.C.E.
Professor C. E. Inglis, O.B.E., M.Inst.C.E.
Colonel Sir John W. Pringle, C.B., R.E. (ret.), M.Inst.C.E.
R. V. Southwell, F.R.S.
E. F. C. Trench, C.B.E., M.Inst.C.E. (L.M.S.R.).

For questions of locomotive design they had the assistance of Sir Henry Fowler, K.B.E., M.Inst.C.E. who became Chief Mechanical Engineer of the L.M.S.R.

The Report of this Committee was published in 1928. It marked a great step forward in the scientific assessment of the true carrying capacity of a railway bridge; it came barely in time because the impact effects with which the bridge engineer has to deal arise from the fact that the motion of a (steam) locomotive is not one of smooth rolling. Prominent in those effects are the periodic variations of rail pressure due to hammer-blow. These variations have no proportionality to the load; they may be far greater in a light locomotive than in a heavy one; in a three- or four-cylinder locomotive they are relatively small, and in an electric locomotive they may be absent. Deprived of the reciprocating steam locomotive, the problem loses most of its complexity; and without the wracking, lurching and hammering effect of the engine the passing of which so many folks deplored to see, many a railway girder bridge has received a reprieve.

Lord Balfour, President of the Council, wrote the Introductory Note to the Report. On the technical side of the question he said he was not competent to speak; nevertheless, the following extract is very apt.

"To those who are not engineers the building of railway bridge may seem a very simple affair. There should be no difficulty, they think, in discovering the maximum weight which the proposed bridge will have to support, and then design a structure strong enough to support it. When these two things have been accomplished, and a margin of safety has been calculated by some rough-and-ready method, the practical problem is supposed to have been solved, and the bridge builder may proceed light-heartedly to complete his enterprise.

"This, however, is a delusion. The problem of bridge building is obviously other than that of providing an adequate support for a stationary load. It is mainly concerned with the business of providing support for a load in motion.

PLATE 28. One of the prefabricated and welded base units for the northern tower of the Forth Road Bridge, showing the internal flanges, machined and larger but otherwise similar to the flanges joining together the top chord units of the 1962 trusses of the Chepstow Bridge.

PLATE 29. Assembling the new Up lines trusses under the "land" spans at Chepstow. (Photo: B.R.)

PLATE 30. En route from Fairfield's workshops to Chepstow Bridge, a completed top chord unit.

PLATE 31. Launching the Up line span at Chepstow. (Photo: B.R.)

PLATE 32. Landed, the Up line span rests safely on its permanent supports at Chepstow.

PLATE 33. Destressing one of the old trusses by jacking down an A-frame strut after gas-cutting out a short length of the wrough tiron, at Chepstow Bridge. (Photo: B.R.)

PLATE 34. The tops of the tubes at Chepstow. The Up line tube almost straight after the truss had been destressed; the workman walks the still cambered Down line tube. (Photo: B.R.)

PLATE 35. The Up line tube about to be lowered on to railway trucks at Chepstow Bridge. (Photo: B.R.)

PLATE 36. The Up line tube at Chepstow almost down. (Photo: B.R.)

PLATE 37. The Down line tube leaving the scene at Chepstow.
(Photo: B.R.)

PLATE 38. The tubes of the Royal Albert Bridge are straight between each
pair of verticals and change direction at the nodal points. A picture taken
from a ladder on the upstream side of the Devon span tube.

This is true of all bridges. It is true, for example, of a plank on which a wheelbarrow is pushed across a ditch. But questions which can be answered empirically when you are dealing with a plank, a man, and a wheelbarrow, become of immense complication and corresponding difficulty when you are designing colossal steel structures to carry enormous loads, dragged at very high and variable speeds by powerful locomotives. Fixed bridges and trains in motion become for brief periods parts of a single mechanical system. . . .

"The importance and difficulty of the problems thus raised are denied by none, but they are not always remembered. The interaction between bridge and locomotive is the root of the whole matter. Yet no maker of locomotives is greatly concerned with the structure of bridges, nor has any builder of bridges possessed adequate opportunities of experimenting with locomotives in motion. The complex relation between the two has therefore never been completely understood. . . ."

Lord Balfour rounded off his Note by saying the railway companies would reap their reward for assisting in the investigations; "but the reward will be shared", he said, "by all those who are interested, whether as travellers or as economists, in the promotion of railway enterprise throughout the world. And this is as it should be."

CHAPTER 23

Looking Both Ways

THE Report of the Bridge Stress Committee in 1928 attracted world-wide attention. Nevertheless, neither the United States nor India, two countries who had their own independent ways of allowing for the effects of impact without taking account of the hammer-blow of particular classes of locomotives, thought fit to adopt these British recommendations. They were not alone with their views. Even in Britain it was not until after nationalization in 1947 that all regions of British Railways started to take notice of the differences between various classes of steam engines so far as they affected bridges and permanent way. Before that, all running permissions throughout the East Coast lines had been authorized on calculations based solely on the axle weights of engines measured while they were standing still.

The Report brought to everyone's notice, civil engineer and mechanical engineer alike, the importance of keeping the magnitude of hammer-blow in check. Even before the ink was dry some of the work had borne fruit. Certain classes of locomotive were modified immediately; the severity of the effects of the unbalanced forces seemed to come as quite a shock to some of the C.M.E.'s. For a while attention was paid to the limiting of the hammer-blow in the design of new engines. But it was only for a while that locomotive designers paid heed to the advantages of using three or four cylinders, rather than two. This particular recommendation made by the Bridge Stress Committee seemed soon to be forgotten. None of the British Railways standard locomotives designed after nationalization had more than two cylinders.

Each of Britain's railways had, in company days, its own system of giving running permissions. Some took note of the effects of impact; some did not. The Great Western had a splendid system by which every engine and every section of the line were classified according to their colour. The colour appeared in small round markings on the sides of the engine cabs and on maps accompanying the working time-tables; so every traffic officer and signalman could tell at a glance if a certain locomotive was authorized to run by a particular route. The colours chosen were red, blue, yellow and "uncoloured". Engines classed as uncoloured could run anywhere; they were the lightest. At the other end of the scale, a red engine could run only on red routes, a blue engine could operate on red and blue routes, but not on yellow or uncoloured lines. "King" class engines were double-red and were permitted only over routes specially noted. Since hammer-blow, and indeed impact effects generally, increase as the square of the speed, engines of a higher colour class were allowed to run over routes of a lower colour capacity when their speed was suitably restricted. For instance, a red 2-cylinder "County" 4-6-0, which had a heavy hammer-blow, was allowed to work trains over certain blue routes provided the speed was kept below prescribed limits over certain bridges. The effect of this ruling often perplexed the amateur railway enthusiast who did not see why, in an emergency, a "County" would lose time with a train normally worked to schedule by a less powerful blue engine.

The findings of the Report worked both ways. The route-availability of the light-weight engine with a heavy hammer-blow was reduced, while well-balanced engines with more than two cylinders had their route-availability increased. The bridge engineer was in a happier position because he could give much wider running permissions where speeds were unlikely to be high enough to make the hammer-blow effect serious on a weak bridge. For example, speed over Sheepwash Bridge at the north end of the platform lines at Oxford station could never be high; so permission could be given for engines of a higher colour to operate across a bridge which, if it had been out in the open country, would have had a colour of a lower category.

The 1923 Bridge Stress Committee, through their research, reduced the gap which had for many years separated practice from theory. The knowledge of stresses actually occurring in girder bridges increased. The margin between the loading permitted across a bridge and the loading which would bring about the downfall of the structure could be assessed more accurately. But it still could not be determined with mathematical exactitude. Even "the downfall of the structure" had a very wide meaning. At one extreme it implied complete collapse; at the other it could mean the start of some minor deformation which could lead to the initiation of a harmless crack. Many thousands of loading cycles, perhaps an infinite number, might lie between these extremes. So much would have to go wrong with a girder bridge before serious structural failure took place. With periodical inspections catastrophic collapse was a practical impossibility. That, of course, is as it should be.

However, the loosening rivet and the hole which might arrest the spread of a crack, are not to be found in a welded bridge. So, to guard against the risk of even the tiniest crack starting to form, the British Standard Specification for Steel Girder Bridges was revised in 1962.

Although no bridge has been known to have failed solely through metal-fatigue (see Chapter 21), the compilers of the new specification were taking no chances. The parts of bridges subjected to fluctuations of stress are described as being liable to suffer from fatigue failure. This, it is claimed, may be caused by loads very much lower than those which would be necessary to cause failure under a single application.

To meet the requirements of this specification, today's designer must first guess—technically the word used is assess!—the numbers and magnitude of stress cycles computed from a traffic forecast over the life period of his bridge. On British Rail the average life period is taken as 120 years, and on a basic main line in a heavy industrial area 75 per cent of the traffic is to be considered as freight and 25 per cent passenger. In London the traffic forecast simply allows for a 15 per cent increase over existing traffic densities.

To arrive at this forecast of stress cycles, the designer must study the current time-tables and, after gazing into the crystal ball, decide how many of the trains will be hauled by the heaviest locomotives, how many will be of multiple-unit passenger stock, how many freights will be loaded, how many empty, and so on. And in the end he must select the permissible stress up to which his bridge may be designed, from tables of figures based on the particular class of constructional detail adopted.

That some tightening up of the bridge specifications was wanted to meet the circumstances occasioned by the introduction of welding, few will deny. But in the light of past experience one wonders if the pendulum may not, in fact, have swung too far the other way. Dozens of welded bridges were built between 1948 and the issue of this new specification, and thousands of riveted steel and wrought iron bridges all over the world have already had more trains across them than would be permitted under these rules for new bridges (and the specification does apply equally to riveted work as well as welded). Perhaps it is not a bad idea to reflect on what Stephenson, Brunel, Fowler or Baker would have done. The designers of the Britannia Tubular, the Royal Albert and the Forth bridges and the many other thousands of girder bridges which are today giving perfectly satisfactory service, certainly never took time off to count how many trains, loaded or empty, were going to cross their bridges.

CHAPTER 24

Closing Down

In Britain railways needed an Act of Parliament before they could be laid down; factories and homes followed where public transport had established the convenience of quick and cheap movement; and once a railway had been so built it is logical that such a service should not be interrupted without public consent. So whether company-owned or a nationalized undertaking, a railway cannot be regarded as being on the same terms as a commercial trader whose very existence depends on profit-making. The question is not how best to make British Rail pay but how best to prolong the twilight existence of a nationalized industry while much needed reforms are sacrificed at the feet of the modern idol, the motor car.

The winds of change have reached gale force in the realm of transport. Fifty years ago it was the exception to meet someone in Britain who had not been in a railway train. Another fifty years on it will be rare to come across a middle-aged resident who will remember a journey behind a steam locomotive. City workers will, no doubt, be familiar with travel by urban rail; but whether the trunk routes will have survived the lopping off of the branches is not so certain. Meanwhile, the engineers have to help solve the problem of what to do with bridges, for which no money is forthcoming for urgently needed repairs, on lines which may or may not be closed in the near future. Sometimes other things take a hand in forcing a decision, and sometimes they are not so unexpected as they seem at the time.

One of the longest bridges on the Western Region was the Severn

Bridge, 4162 ft, across the fearsome waters and sandbanks of the estuary between Lydney on the west and Sharpness on the east. It was built to enable coal from the Forest of Dean to be brought by rail to ocean-going ships loading at Sharpness which were too large to negotiate the Gloucester & Berkeley Canal. Construction of the bridge started in March 1875, and under the joint ownership of the Severn & Wye and Severn Bridge Companies, it was opened for traffic on 17 October 1879. On 25 October 1960, within two years of a decision having been taken to strengthen the girderwork at a cost of more than £108,000, the Severn Bridge was closed for all time. One of its twenty cast iron piers had been knocked down by a couple of self-propelled oil-barges drifting up river on the in-coming tide, out of control and lost in the swirling mists that frequent this part of the river in autumn. Five of the eight men on the barges lost their lives; and the railway lost about five miles of line which had never been prosperous, had brought its original owners to the verge of bankruptcy four years after the bridge had been opened, and in 1960 served only to enable school-children in Sharpness to attend classes in Lydney, to carry an important gas-main across the river, and to give an alternative route for a few South Wales trains on Sundays during the winter when the Severn Tunnel is regularly closed for maintenance. From the headlines in the national press it looked as though the collision between the ships and the bridge was the kind of mishap which ought never to have been expected. Yet the accident was just the kind of thing forseen in 1865 when Sir John Fowler's scheme for a two-mile long "Chepstow" bridge across the Severn below Sharpness (see Chapter 12) was looked upon with disfavour because of "its impediment to navigation".

Fowler's bridge would have been directly across the channel used by ocean-going ships *below* Sharpness. The Severn Bridge was less than half a mile *above* the entrance to Sharpness docks and the canal for which the ill-fated barges were making their way on the evening of 25 October 1960. Half a mile is a short enough distance to a captain who has lost his way in dense fog and is being swept along in a 4-knot current.

To go back to the beginning of the Severn Bridge. George William Keeling of Lydney and G. W. Owen of Westminster were the engineers, with Thomas E. Harrison, President of The Institution of Civil Engineers (1873), consulting. Counting from the Sharpness end of the bridge, there were the following wrought iron bowstring girder spans:

1 swing span 197 ft long across the canal,
13 spans of 134 ft 6 in.,
5 spans of 171 ft,
2 spans of 327 ft over the navigable river channel, and
1 span of 134 ft.

With the exception of the swing span which had a width of 24 ft 6 in., all were built to carry a single line of 4 ft 8½ in. gauge railway.

The superstructure was constructed to give a rise of 1 in 140 towards Lydney, and it gave a headway of 70 ft at high water under the two longest spans. The piers were of cast iron cylinders varying between 6 and 7 ft in diameter above low water level, and 9 and 10 ft in diameter below. There were four of these cylinders in each of the three piers carrying the navigation spans; all the others had two cylinders and they were braced together with cast iron frames. In all there were 3528 tons of wrought iron in the girderwork, and above low water 2171 tons of cast iron in the pier cylinders which were filled with 4321 yd³ of lime concrete. Another 1500 tons of cast iron was buried in the sands and went down to rock 70 ft below high water level.

The contractors were the Hamilton Windsor Iron Works Co., Ltd. of Liverpool, and the cost was £190,000.

The Severn Bridge was built at a time when many other great structures were being erected; but it is doubtful whether any bridge could have been across a more treacherous estuary than the Severn. And it was a form of construction which left the contractor with no alternative to building falsework all the way across the river, and then putting the iron girderwork together on top of this temporary timber bridge. Second only to the Bay of Fundy in North America, the Severn tidal range at Sharpness exceeds 40 ft; and, during the flow, the tide rises 27 ft in 3 hours.

The cast iron cylinders were made in lengths of 4 ft, and *Engineering* dated 24 October 1879 records that during the machining of the internal flanges, by which the 4-ft lengths were to be eventually joined together, the cylinders were "turned in a lathe and tooled at both ends at once". During sinking, the cylinders were weighted with 150 tons of ballast; men had to work down below inside the cylinders where they were subjected to pneumatic pressures between 5 and 40 lb/in². The air-locks used were the same as used at Bouch's Tay Bridge; and according to a contemporary issue of *The Engineer* a workman inside one of the cylinders had a remarkable escape from death when he fell 70 ft: "His arm was broken in the fall, but otherwise he was only slightly hurt, and was soon at work again."

Another remarkable thing about the cylinders of the Severn Bridge was the use of felt as a lining between the cast iron and the concrete. Intended to prevent the cast iron from cracking, the idea did not meet with the success the engineers had hoped for; by 1960 there was hardly a cylinder in the whole length of the bridge which had not been cracked by frost. But although the felt was a failure, it is interesting to review the reasoning behind the idea. *The Engineer* wrote:

> "The felt was employed as a compressible medium between the cast iron and the concrete to allow for the difference between the expansion and contraction of iron and concrete. The difference between the expansion of cast iron and the materials constituting the concrete, is not very great between the limits of temperature likely to be met with on the Severn. Between 32 degrees Fah. and 212, the average coefficient of expansion of cast iron is 0·000,06,16 for 1 degree, while that of cement, slate, granite, stock-bricks and sandstone may be taken as 0·000,005,3. The greater range of expansion and contraction of iron for equal increments and decrement of temperature will thus only tend to injure the cylinders during contraction, and that only under decrease of temperature which does not take place slowly. The iron being but a thin skin on the enclosed body of concrete, it rapidly gives up its heat under change of temperature, and though probably most of the heat of the concrete passes out from the sides of the cylinder, this only takes place when the iron is at a lower temperature; the cast iron would therefore be liable to severe tensile strains at low temperatures were it not for the lining of felt. The difference in the specific heat of iron and concrete is moreover favourable to more rapid changes of dimensions in the iron."

The contractor encountered trouble in sinking the cylinders of the pier in the navigable channel, one complete length of cast iron being scoured out and the cylinder toppling over. That was not all. Two whole spans of girderwork fell over when some of the temporary falsework was swept away by an incoming tide; and eventually more than 60,000 ft³ of timber had to be used to support the two largest spans, and the work had to be pressed on with all haste, the men working through the nights by electric light "provided by the Pyramid Electric Light Company".

At the opening in 1879 the Severn Bridge was vested in the joint care of the Great Western Railway and the Midland Railway. Subsequently, it was looked after successively by the M.R., the London Midland & Scottish Railway, the London Midland Region of British Railways, and from 11 July 1948 the Western Region of B.R. Throughout its history this bridge had constituted a hazard to shipping; between 1939 and 1961 it was run into by vessels out of control no fewer than seven times. In fact, the pier involved in the accident in October 1960 had been hit by a dumb barge carrying 400 tons of grain in October 1943; and that crash had been so serious that the blow had completely sheared six of the bolts which held the fixed bearings to the topmost castings of the cylinders, and shattered the cast iron bracing framework between the two cylinders from top to bottom. The L.M.S. engineers repaired the pier in due course and substituted mild steel bracings strapped and bolted to the cylinders. However, it is significant that in the report about the damage no mention is made of any fracturing of the cast iron at the base of the cylinders, or of any disturbance to the foundations although the blow which severed six one-inch bolts at the top of the pier could have been enough to have broken the cast iron all around the bases of both cylinders. Apparently, the bridge was considered to have suffered no other damage; so rail traffic, yellow and uncoloured engines with a speed restriction of 15 miles an hour, was restored. But as subsequent events were to show, the bridge must have been a good deal less safe than was supposed. Evidently, those who had turned down Fowler's scheme in 1865 knew what they were talking about.

Stress measurements were made under coupled red "Castle" locomotives in 1957 to determine if heavier engines could be allowed to work between Lydney and Sharpness. Although the stresses recorded near the middle of the diagonal web members were lower than the calculated maxima, the readings near the single lap connections to the bottom chords showed stresses nearly three times as great as the mean in the 132-ft spans, and 50 per cent higher than the mean in the 312-ft spans. These tests were conducted by the Research Department of the British Transport Commission, and Tom Baldwin in the Report said he thought that red engines working across the bridge with a frequency of four trips a week could be expected to bring failure to the diagonal web members after about fourteen years. Understandably, permission for running red engines was not given. But such was the convenience of the Severn Bridge as an escape route when the Severn Tunnel was closed, that the matter was not allowed to drop. A scheme was got out for strengthening the bridge by substituting diagonal web members carrying primary compressive stresses instead of the double system of ties or tension diagonals. This would have eliminated the offending eccentric connections, and the bridge would have been expected to give satisfactory service under red engines at restricted speed for at least fifty years.

A contract was let to Fairfields to carry out the modifications to the web members of all the forty-two main girders of the fixed spans, and to change the badly grooved roller expansion bearings with rubber-cum-steel sandwich blocks. The work was more than halfway through when the crash came which was to put paid to the Severn railway bridge, once and for all.

On the bridge the alterations to the main girders and the bearings could, of course, be carried out only during complete occupations by the engineers when the line was closed to trains. This fact may have been allowed to influence quite wrongly those responsible for the future of the line, for they decided that the remaining £50,000 worth of work still required for the strengthening should be completed. With the bridge closed to trains through the collapse of a pier and two spans, the chance of getting on with the work without interruption seemed a heaven-sent opportunity. But it was a wrong decision. The cost of restoring the bridge was going to cost British Railways more than £250,000 and they were not going to be entitled to anything like that sum in compensation from the owners of the barges which had wrecked the bridge. Not even the most optimistic traffic forecast could justify such an expenditure.

At the time it did seem hard luck on British Railways because it was hardly their fault that a couple of barges should have knocked out their bridge. Or was it? If the bridge had not been there, perhaps the barges would not have sunk!

On the evening of 25 October 1960, the mists swirling about the Severn estuary became quite dense as darkness closed in about the self-propelled steel barges *Wastdale* and *Arkendale*. They were bound for Gloucester and both masters were groping their way up river in the hope of making the entrance to Sharpness docks at high water when the lock-gates would be opened.

The *Wastdale* was loaded with motor spirit in bulk; her all-up weight was 450 tons. The *Arkendale* with a bulk cargo of fuel-oil had an all-up weight of 408 tons. Somewhere off Sharpness Point and shortly before 22.30 hours, the two vessels came together. It was not so much as a collision, they just drifted quietly into contact and became locked together side by side, neither master aware they had drifted past the dock entrance. Almost immediately afterwards the mass of 858 tons struck pier 17 at a speed of between 3½ and 4 knots; an explosion and fire followed; and drifting free of the pitching stone which surrounded the base of the bridge pier, both vessels, still locked together, floated up river nearly a mile before they settled down on a sandbank.

One might have expected that the owners of the barges would have been held responsible for paying the railway the cost of mending the bridge; but it was not so. Had the bridge been wrecked by fire, lightning or explosion, British Railways could have expected claims to be settled for any amount up to a limit of £1½ million; but under the 1956 Merchant Shipping Act the limited liability for making good damage caused through collision did not exceed a sterling sum equal to about twenty-four times the net registered tonnage of the vessel, or as in this case vessels, involved.

Subsequent examination of the remains of the girderwork brought down when the pier fell, and of the two barges, showed quite conclusively that the vessels must have struck the bridge before the so-called explosion occurred. The collision had knocked over the pier; and, seconds later, the impact of the falling girderwork had caused the motor spirit to ignite. Actually, neither the vessels nor the remains of the girders showed any signs of having been damaged by an explosion; witnesses at the enquiry had spoken of an explosion, but what they had seen must have been the almost instantaneous ignition of the highly inflammable cargoes.

British Railways had lost their Severn Bridge by a matter of seconds!

The bridge had been hit so many times in the past; there was no guarantee the same thing would not happen again. It is true that puny timber fenders had been slung from the bridge at piers 18, 19 and 20 near the recognized navigation channel; but they were not very strong, and the cost of substantial protection to those piers and many others besides was considered to be prohibitive. The effects of 858 tons striking pier 17 at a speed of less than 4 knots had been quite bad enough; it gave a warning of what might happen if a similar collision were to take place at half-tide when the water rushes past in a 10-knot mill-race. And the possibility that a train might be crossing the bridge during a repeat performance does not bear thinking about.

No. The bridging of the Severn at Sharpness was not a success story. The loss of a bridge which was both an impediment to shipping and a liability to its owners was a blessing in disguise.

It took British Railways more than six years to make up their mind to get rid of the Severn Bridge—the bridge over which the G.W.R. was granted permission to run four trains each way via the Severn Bridge, the first continuous passenger service between Bristol and South Wales, in 1881 after fire had devastated Portskewett pier and put the Severn ferry service out of action on Sunday 22 May—and to find a contractor willing to undertake the removal of the girderwork and the dismantling of the piers down as far as low water level. Eventually, in the spring of 1967, the Nordman Construction Co. of Gloucester were entrusted with the contract. For £75,000, this firm agreed to dismantle and remove the Severn Bridge including the masonry arches on the approaches; and they were to be free to either sell the whole of the ironwork for use elsewhere or to realize its value as scrap.

CHAPTER 25

Clearing Up

CRUMLIN Viaduct was another great bridge which was too weak to carry on. It could have been strengthened but only at a cost estimated to be at least a quarter of a million pounds; the potential traffic did not justify such an expenditure. So the loftiest bridge in South Wales was closed to traffic in 1964, and a contract was let to Bird & Co. for the removal of 1300 tons of wrought iron and 1250 tons of cast iron. The bridge was taken down in 1965–6.

Crumlin Viaduct carried the Taff Vale extension of the Newport Abergavenny & Hereford Railway across Ebbw Vale. In 1860 the N.A. & H.R. became part of the West Midland; and in 1863 it became G.W.R. Built between 1853 and 1857, the viaduct consisted of ten 150-ft spans supported on open cross-braced cast iron pillars forming the piers. It was in fact two bridges, a short length of line across a shoulder of a hill dividing the structure into two. The longer part had seven spans and had a maximum height from the underside of the foundations to the top of the handrailing of 208 ft.

All the spans were identical. Each consisted of four similar underslung pin-jointed wrought iron girders trussed according to the then newly patented Warren system. Crumlin Viaduct was in fact the first large bridge to be built on the Warren principle, and its construction marked an important step in the development of the prefabricated bridge designed on mass-production lines; in fact, like Brunel's bridge over the Wye at Chepstow, Crumlin Viaduct led to the setting up of a bridge-fabricator's works on the site and, subsequently, to the export of girderwork to many parts of the world.

The trussed girders at Crumlin belonged to a family of bridge beams which are often referred to as lattice girders. Actually, this is a misnomer. Properly, a lattice girder is one having many diagonal web members resembling lattice-work or trellis. Girders built on the Warren system have only a single system of diagonals, and in elevation they look like a series of "W"s, sometimes with verticals like the new trusses of the modern Chepstow Bridge. In the Warren truss, adjacent diagonal members alternate like the strokes of a "W"; they are not to be confused with the Pratt truss in which all the diagonals each side of the middle of the girder are parallel so that the girder looks like a succession of "Ns". Technically, in a Warren truss the diagonals alternate between ties or tension members, and struts; in a Pratt truss they are usually all ties though towards the centre of the span they will have to be formed like struts so as to carry the compressive stresses which occur there under certain loading conditions.

The truss girder was popular in North America where early railroads made use of timber for the strut members and wrought iron bars for the ties. Timber was plentiful and the bars did not take up much room on board ship; so it is easy to see why the Pratt truss was used extensively in the United States in pioneering days. But there were practical difficulties in making sound and lasting joints between the members, and the maintenance of some of the early forms of truss girder bridges was to prove costly and often extremely troublesome. At one period truss girder bridges on the railroads in the United States were failing at a rate of 27 every 12 months.

During the Enquiry into the Use of Iron in Railway Bridges held in 1847, several of the witnesses, Robert Stephenson included, spoke against the use of truss girders for railways because of the difficulty of looking after framework which was apt to shake loose under the "concussions". And from an examination of the accompanying sketch of part of an 86-ft long truss used in the Ballysimon Bridge on the Waterford & Limerick Railway, it is not difficult to see that Stephenson had very good reasons for his statement. The sketch has been taken from the 1847 Report which states that the bridge "sunk $\frac{5}{16}$ in. when tested with a weight of 80 tons, by the Inspector of Railways".

According to Eric de Maré in his *The Bridges of Britain*, published by B. T. Batsford, London, 1954, the first use of lattice girders made of wrought iron in the British Isles was in a 40-foot span occupation

WATERFORD & LIMERICK RAILWAY.

BALLYSIMON BRIDGE.

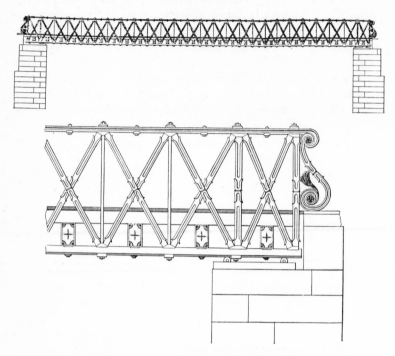

Fig. 18. A drawing of a 50-ft long bridge on the Waterford & Limerick Railway, exhibited at the 1847 Enquiry. Small wonder that "several of the witnesses spoke against the use of truss girders for railways. . . ".

road bridge across a cutting on a railway line between Dublin and Drogheda. The design was attributed to Sir John M'Neile and the date was 1842, well before the "Warren" truss was patented by James Warren and Willoughby Theobald Monzani in August 1848 (*Proc. Inst. C.E.*, vol. XII, 1852–3).

The very first underline bridge using Warren truss girders in Britain appears to have been on the Great Northern Railway. There were two separate structures, one for the Down line and one for the Up, carrying the main line over a branch of the River Trent near Newark. Known as the Newark Dyke Bridge, there were two through type Warren

PLATE 39. Testing Chepstow Bridge. One of the last duties performed by "King Henry VI" and "King James I" before they were withdrawn from service.

PLATE 40. Time marches on at Runcorn-Widnes. William Baker's 305-ft lattice girder spans have been carrying trains since 1848. Under erection, the 1082-ft arch road bridge opened in July 1961.

PLATE 41. Part of John J. Webster's transporter bridge at Runcorn before it was closed and taken away in 1962.

PLATE 42. Bailey bridging being used to dismantle the trusses at the Crumlin Viaduct. (Photo: B.R.)

PLATE 43. The Severn Bridge (railway) after pier 17 and two 171-ft spans had been knocked down in October 1960. (Photo: B.R.)

PLATE 44. One of the Crumlin Viaduct piers being felled by winching over. (Photo: B.R.)

PLATE 45. The effect of running an out-of-balance locomotive at speed. The deformed rails are having to be taken out of the track. (Photo: B.R.)

PLATE 46. Penryn Viaduct (1863–1934) was typical of Brunel's cheap bridging in the early days of railways. Prosperity and dividends were expected to follow. The timbers in these "spider" bridges lasted between 27 and 30 years and an experienced bridge-gang could renew any one of the parts within one hour. (Photo: B.R.)

PLATE 47. Technically, the world's most advanced bridge yet built. Sixty feet of prefabricated deck carrying two 24-ft carriageways, a footpath and a cycle-track, goes up in a single operation during the construction of the Severn Road Bridge in 1965.

truss girder spans, each with a clear span of 240 ft 6 in. A Paper read before The Institution of Civil Engineers in 1852 by Joseph Cubitt attributes the design to Charles Wild. In the girders all members subjected to compressive strains were made of cast iron, and all ties were of wrought iron. In one span there were $138\frac{1}{4}$ tons of cast iron, and $106\frac{1}{4}$ tons of wrought iron; and under a test load of five of the heaviest G.N.R. locomotives, the central deflection was $2\frac{1}{2}$ in. The builders of the bridge were Fox & Henderson and the cost of the girderwork including erection is said to have been £20 per ton. Robert Stephenson spoke during a discussion on Cubitt's Paper and he gave it as his considered opinion that "plates for a tubular bridge would be found to be more portable".

Newark Dyke Bridge had been brought into use in 1850. So its designer was a contemporary of Isambard Brunel working on his Chepstow Bridge and of Fairbairn and Robert Stephenson with their Conway and Britannia Tubular Bridges. It was a time when far-sighted engineers were searching for the girder made entirely of wrought iron to the total exclusion of cast iron; and it was on these lines that Thomas Kennard was thinking when he produced his Warren truss girders, wholly of prefabricated riveted wrought iron members joined together with wrought iron pins, for Crumlin Viaduct.

Actually, Kennard was the contractor whose design for Crumlin Viaduct was selected by Liddell, engineer to the N.A. & H. Railway Company. Kennard had a foundry at Falkirk, and all the 1250 tons of cast iron used in the piers came from Scotland. But the wrought iron came from the Blaenavon Iron Co. in South Wales; in the twenty pairs of girders and bracings of the superstructure, 880 tons, and in the piers another 260 tons. All turning, boring and fitting work was done in a works built adjacent to the site of the viaduct where the facilities for fabricating and riveting the wrought iron girderwork were to establish the then new industry of bridge manufacture.

The valley crossed by the longer part of the viaduct had at the bottom a bed of alluvial soil, chiefly hard gravel which was considered adequate to support the foundations of those piers not actually on virgin rock. In this valley there already existed the Western Valleys Railway and the navigation canal of the Monmouthshire Railway & Canal Company which gave communication with the port of Newport and the Ebbw river. The canal was stopped off and the bed excavated for the foundations of the tallest pier which was to become known as the Isabella Pier. These foundations consisted of 12 in. of concrete formed on the gravel and overlaid with a 4-in. course of Memel timber planks; and on top of this layer of timber 12 ft of solid masonry formed the base on which the cast iron pillars were bolted down. The use of the timber sandwich is interesting.

Kennard and Liddell were certainly not averse to the benefits of publicity; no doubt the former knew the value of advertisement. The day appointed for erecting the first piece of cast iron pillar at the base of the tallest pier was 8 December 1853; and the formality of declaring the pillar well and truly laid was performed by Lady Isabella Fitzmaurice, who, "in the presence of the Directors, several of the gentry of the neighbourhood, and persons interested in the work, placed beneath it, in a recess in the stone, a cup containing coins of the current date, after which the permanent bolts were put in, and the work formally commenced. A bottle of wine was broken over the spot, and this pier was called the Isabella Pier." The cup bore the inscription:

"Crumlin Viaduct. This column was erected by the Hon. Captain Fitzmaurice, chairman, assisted by the Hon. Mrs Fitzmaurice, Lady Isabella Fitzmaurice, and T. W. Kennard, Esq. December 8, 1853."

The final completion of the viaduct in May 1857, the momentous month and year of the Indian Mutiny, was certainly not allowed to pass off without publicity. The day chosen was Whit-Monday, and according to one contemporary writer 20,000 persons were present throughout the day "and cannon were placed on both sides of the valley, from which volleys were fired with but slight intermission throughout the day, and caused the mountains to reverberate with their thunder".

Certainly, Crumlin Viaduct was something to shout about. Fifteen hundred feet of double-track railway bridge, 200 ft high near the middle, had been built for an all-in cost, including masonry, of only £62,000, or about £41 7s. 0d. per foot run. It was cheap; it was light; but it was only just adequate for the traffic of the day. Kennard had won the contract in competition with other designers; he did not allow for any growth in future loading, and he did not pay much attention to the protection of the wrought ironwork against rusting.

In the beginning, Crumlin Viaduct was decked over with creosoted Baltic timber, 6 in. thick and forming a platform 26 ft wide between the handrailings. One pair of the girders had been tested before erection, under a distributed load of 230 tons; Edwin Clark of Menai Bridge fame was present at the test, and the deflection at the centre was $1\frac{1}{2}$ in. Each girder was only 9 in. wide. So before being braced to another to form a pair, a single girder was extremely whippy. The first one had been hoisted aloft and even landed safely on the piers; but when the second girder was being lifted it folded up under its own weight, killing an unfortunate workman who was riding the girder as it was being hoisted aloft.

Before the Crumlin Viaduct was opened to traffic it was tested in the presence of Colonel Wynne, the Board of Trade Inspector. The test load was six heavy locomotive engines, "each of which was increased in weight by filling up all available space on them with pig iron, making the weight of each engine 50 tons, and making a total weight of 300 tons, which was just enough to cover one span on both lines of rails". Thus the test load per foot run of track was 1 ton only, or less than half the test loading Brunel used on his broad-gauge lines across the Chepstow Bridge. The N.A. & H.R. was, of course, 4 ft $8\frac{1}{2}$ in. gauge.

Under the six test engines the deflections of the Crumlin spans varied between $\frac{7}{8}$ and $1\frac{1}{4}$ in. according as the speed was increased upwards from a crawl. The maximum speed during those tests is not recorded; but it cannot have been much over 40 miles an hour at the most, and the variations in the deflection readings is very large and shows the spans were very "lively".

The timber decking lasted until 1868 when it was replaced with a wrought iron plate floor carried on cross-girders. It would not have been so bad if these new cross-beams had been located over the panel points but they were not. And to make matters worse, this new flooring was riveted to all four girders in each span; the cross-girders were not nearly strong enough to stand the effects of the unequal deflection as one pair of girders bent down under the weight of a train while the other pair under an empty track tried to stay more or less level. Added to this wracking of the iron floor there was a natural tendency for the plating to act as a top chord common to all four girders. Bridge engineers call this floor-interaction; and, unless the structure has been specially designed to behave in this way, it is not a good thing. When the floor is made continuous from end to end of the span and it is the part of the ironwork furthest from the neutral axis, it is logical to find that floor trying to do the work of the chords of the main girders. At Crumlin floor-interaction was certainly not a good thing. Besides, the contractor who put the viaduct up in the first place had won the work in open competition. He made the girders as light as he possibly could, and in doing so he disregarded all thought for the preservation of the iron during the future maintenance. Neither the insides of the boxes forming the top chords which were open at each nodal point, nor the inter-sections of the web members with the bottom chords could be got at with a paint brush.

So, from the beginning, Crumlin had no reserve of strength. Once corrosion took hold there was little that could be done to prolong its life except by restricting the loading the viaduct had to carry. The two tracks were replaced by a single line laid down the centre in 1927. But even so, loading had to be restricted to "dotted" blue engines which means that certain blue engines were prohibited altogether. For in-stance, the standard British Railways 2-10-0, a blue engine, was allowed to work trains across Crumlin Viaduct; but the same engine made heavier by the fitting of a mechanical stoker was forbidden. The speed of all trains was restricted to not more than 8 miles an hour.

In about 1950 a scheme was got out for reconstructing the whole of the superstructure. The piers being mainly of cast iron had suffered hardly any deterioration, and it seemed that the viaduct could be brought up to full strength if the girders and decking were replaced with modern steelwork. It would still have been restricted to a single-line bridge, but the speed restriction could have been lifted. The scheme came to nothing, however, because the traffic potential did not justify the expenditure which would have been well over £100,000. So the decision was taken to close the line within ten years.

It cost British Railways £41,750 to get rid of Crumlin Viaduct. The contractors who took away the girders used a temporary "erection" span of Bailey bridging to support the old superstructure as the trusses were cut into pieces and lowered to the ground. They had hoped to have been able to take down each truss complete; but, like the erectors, they were to learn their lesson. A slim and slender girder with a length-to-width ratio of 200 is liable to buckle under its own weight. The first one to be taken down crumpled up, fortunately without causing injury to any personnel.

Getting the piers down was no problem; they were simply pulled over by a rope wound in by a winch, and afterwards it was only a matter of cutting up the parts which had not been smashed in the fall, and carting the bits off to the scrap merchant. There was an air of expectancy following the demolition of Lady Isabella's pier; but, alas, neither cup nor coins were found.

Crumlin Viaduct lasted well over 100 years, but with a much reduced capacity. As wrought iron bridges go, this was not particularly good; Conway, the Britannia Tubular, and the Royal Albert bridges have all passed their century and with careful maintenance and no ill-treatment through over-loading, they should give a good many more years' service. Generally, the bigger bridges last longer than the short ones. There are two reasons for this. Firstly, the longer the span is, the greater will be the proportion of stress due to holding itself up and the less will be the changes in stress as a train runs across the bridge. Secondly, size has a psychological effect on those responsible for looking after a bridge; no one would take much notice if an insignificant looking plate girder span was allowed to rust and get into a shabby state, but there would be a public outcry if ever the Forth Bridge were neglected.

During the reign of steam, bridges of wrought iron and mild steel suffered ill-effects from the exhaust gases and the out-of-balance forces of the reciprocating motion. In 1947 one out of every three underline girder bridges was more than eighty years old (*Proc. Inst. C.E.* vol. XVIII, April 1961); by 1963 the average age was increasing by about 6 months in every year and that figure was very definitely on the increase. In fact, with the elimination of the rail-joint through the use of continuous welded rails, and the demise of the steam locomotive, British Rail now look forward to getting much longer service from their girder bridges with greatly reduced maintenance costs.

Nevertheless, a bridge is a fixed asset and provision has to be allowed for in the maintenance and depreciation over the assumed period during which it will carry its load economically either with or without restriction. In the past, many bridges built of riveted steelwork lasted only between forty and sixty years and their annual upkeep cost amounted to a figure between 0·6 and 1·0 per cent of the capital cost; the modern welded girder bridge designed so that every part can be got at and painted, will last much longer and cost very much less to maintain. But no bridge will last for ever if it is not looked after. The capacity of a railway line is conditional on speed, train length, rates of acceleration and braking, the signalling system and the strength of the permanent way and the formation. Any weak bridge which restricts loading or speed detracts from the commercial value of the railway. And so deciding whether to repair or to reconstruct a bridge depends upon which course is the more economical, taking into account losses due to restricted working because of its condition and the cost involved in raising the money to pay for reconstruction if and when it becomes inevitable. The solution to the question involves estimations of the remaining life of the bridge, the future requirements of the railway, and the probable value of sterling in the future. Operations which are not entirely removed from the art of looking into a crystal ball!

It is extremely rare for a railway bridge to make a good road bridge. Like the iron roads they were designed to carry, railway girder bridges are usually too narrow and too restricted. Before the great suspension road bridges spanned the Tamar, Forth and Severn, proposals were made for accommodating roadways on the Royal Albert, the Forth and the Severn railway bridges. On Brunel's bridge at Saltash, a road along the ballasted single-track railway was nothing more than a wartime measure. But across the Forth, serious consideration was given in 1948 to a scheme put forward by Sir Bruce White, Wolfe Barry & Partners. They proposed an independent roadway deck, 18 ft wide with two foot-ways each 30 in. wide, above the railway. It would have been cheaper than building a separate road bridge; and, in the event of the railway north of Edinburgh being abandoned, it would have given two 18 ft wide carriageways. Some may think this a poor return for the more limited expenditure in taking the road across the Firth of Forth at Queensferry, and certainly it is hardly to be compared with the two 24 ft carriageways of the magnificent road bridge which Her Majesty Queen Elizabeth II opened on 4 September 1964; but until the Ministry was able to find the funds for the new road bridge, Sir Bruce White's idea was not without merit, even though it would have spoiled the appearance of Sir Benjamin Baker's bridge.

A road across the ¾-mile long single-track Severn Bridge had been considered more than once before that bridge was put out of action in 1960. But it would have been of very limited capacity; the width of the carriageway would have restricted road traffic to a single lane.

Of course, there have been exceptions. Abroad, the mighty Quebec

Bridge with its longest railway span in the world, has long since lost one of its two railway tracks in making room for a roadway.

But the railway girder bridge is seldom capable of giving any greater flexibility in service than the railroad it carries. For the most part, the ironmongery of the Victorian transport system has no place in the modern highway of today; and as more and more railway lines come to be closed, the monuments to Stephenson, Brunel, Arrol and the other great engineers of the nineteenth century will disappear.

Index